QUAKE
DOGS

QUAKE DOGS

Heart-warming stories
of Christchurch dogs

TEXT BY
LAURA SESSIONS

PHOTOGRAPHY BY
CRAIG BULLOCK

RANDOM HOUSE
NEW ZEALAND

A RANDOM HOUSE BOOK published by Random House New Zealand
18 Poland Road, Glenfield, Auckland, New Zealand

For more information about our titles go to www.randomhouse.co.nz

A catalogue record for this book is available from the National Library
of New Zealand

Random House New Zealand is part of the Random House Group
New York   London   Sydney   Auckland   Delhi   Johannesburg

First published 2013, Reprinted 2013, 2014.

© 2013 text, Laura Sessions; images, Craig Bullock (www.furtography.co.nz)
except p10 (top), p12 (top left and bottom) Laura Sessions, p12 (top right)
Chris Turner

The moral rights of the author have been asserted

ISBN 978 1 77553 408 2

Design: Carla Sy
Cover photograph: Craig Bullock

Printed in China by Everbest Printing Co Ltd

To George and Mildred,
the original Quake Dogs.

Contents

Introduction

We have all heard many stories about the effects of the 2010 and 2011 Canterbury earthquakes on people's lives and our city's buildings and infrastructure. But how have these dramatic events changed the lives of our animals? This book gives a dog's perspective on the various ways the earthquakes have altered canine lives, for better and worse, in Christchurch and beyond.

We have been amazed at people's willingness to tell us their dogs' stories, and to share their own experiences during the major quakes of 4 September 2010, 22 February 2011, 13 June 2011 and 23 December 2011 — not to mention the 11,000-odd aftershocks. Many of these people have suffered illness and anxiety; they have lost homes, jobs and even loved ones. Their generosity in sharing their stories says much about New Zealanders' devotion to their dogs. Their stories have brought us a few tears and, in true Christchurch spirit, much laughter and joy.

From the many stories we have heard, our overwhelming sense is that during these difficult times, our dogs have been as much a comfort to us as we have been to them. The intensity of the earthquake experience has heightened that wordless connection between people and their dogs. Through life-or-death experiences, we have become more observant of them, and likewise they have reflected our own emotions back to us.

Through the earthquakes, we have gone to extraordinary lengths to

Their stories have brought us a few tears and, in true Christchurch spirit, much laughter and joy.

ensure our dogs are safe and healthy. People have spent thousands on vet bills and anti-anxiety treatments. Some have even made the ultimate sacrifice and re-homed their dogs outside of Christchurch for the good of their pets. Charities such as Helping You Help Animals (HUHA), K9 Rescue and Rehoming, and Dogwatch took in hundreds of lost and distraught animals, reuniting them with their owners when possible and re-homing those that were not so fortunate.

Of course, dogs went to extra-ordinary lengths for us, too. In particular, the New Zealand Fire Service Urban Search and Rescue (USAR) dogs and their dedicated handlers worked relentlessly to find survivors in the aftermath of the 22 February quake.

In our quest for the best quake dog stories, there is hardly a suburb in Christchurch that we haven't visited. Further afield, we have also visited dogs around the Canterbury region, from Ashburton to Rangiora and Glentunnel to Oxford. We have even travelled to Auckland, Dunedin, Wellington and Oamaru, all to help us try to understand the unique experiences of dogs during the unusual events of the past few years.

During the interviews and photo shoots, we have been licked half to death, battered and bruised by dogs who were so pleased to see us, pooped on by three-week-old puppies and hidden in holes for dogs to find at USAR training. We had a dog try to eat the camera and another land on it while trying to catch a ball. We had more than one run-in with our GPS navigation system, especially when it sent us on the windiest and narrowest road we have ever seen, from Otaki to Upper Hutt.

If we had a dollar for every time someone said 'you'll never get a good

photo of my dog' or 'my dog is afraid of the camera', it's fair to say that we would have a nice retirement fund by now. Luckily, dogs take bribes. Our secret weapons have been over a kilogram of dog treats and many squeaky toys — which had a habit of squeaking at the most inappropriate times, such as while going through airport security or during sombre moments in an interview.

We hope the images and stories contained within this book do justice to the incredible range of experiences that dogs have had during the Canterbury quakes, and that they go some way to show off the characters we have met on this incredible journey.

We are very happy that part of the proceeds from this book will help support one of the organisations that helped to save many dogs following the earthquakes. HUHA is a national organisation that works to rescue and re-home animals around the country, and they came to Christchurch not once, but three times to take more than 70 dogs and numerous other animals to safe and loving homes elsewhere in the country. We are proud to be able to give something back on behalf of Christchurch's quake dogs.

Laura Sessions and Craig Bullock
Christchurch, 2013

Boss

An incredibly fast and almost manic border collie, Boss was 14 months old when Brenda, the national trainer for Urban Search and Rescue (USAR) dogs, adopted him from the Christchurch pound. Boss had spent his life so far locked in a yard, running up and down in pursuit of the cars and motorbikes that drove past all day.

Brenda was asked by Boss's owners whether he was a candidate for re-homing, as he had no obedience or social skills. She recognised his incredible drive and decided to give him a month of training in search and rescue. Within six months, Boss was certified and became a fully operational USAR dog. His intensive training included searching for volunteers hidden in piles of rubble amid confusion and noise — experiences that would help prepare him for the biggest search-and-rescue mission in New Zealand's history.

On 22 February 2011, Boss was one of the first dogs to arrive at the collapsed and burning CTV building, about two and a half hours after the big earthquake. Like all USAR dogs in New Zealand, Boss had been trained to locate people who are alive and buried under rubble by scent, and to then alert his handler by barking frantically.

Just as they arrived at the CTV site, searchers were pulling two people out of the rubble. Boss began searching on that side of the building, where a fire had broken out, and he quickly barked

to indicate that someone was there. On the other side of the site, where the building had collapsed, he barked to alert Brenda again.

In training, Boss would have been rewarded for finding someone with his special search toy, presented by the hidden person. This time, though, Boss did not get to stick around long enough to see whether anyone would emerge from the rubble, as he and Brenda had to race off to another site where they were needed.

However, when they came back to the CTV building later that day, someone said to Brenda, 'You know where the dogs barked at that corner? They got several people out of there. Well done.'

Boss and the other USAR dogs not only helped to locate people who could be rescued, they also kept hope alive for those who were buried and waiting to be found. After the quakes, once Brenda and Boss resumed their weekly Saturday walks, they frequently encountered a man walking a Dalmatian. One day Brenda started talking with him and discovered he had been trapped in the PGC building during the February earthquake. He told Brenda the one thing that kept him going was hearing a dog barking and knowing rescuers were out there looking for him.

The one thing that kept him going was hearing a dog barking.

Loki & Hunny

When the 4 September 2010 earthquake struck, Loki, a nine-year-old keeshond, and Hunny, an eight-year-old border collie, were outside in their kennel in Bexley. Their entire yard and the whole street quickly began to fill with liquefaction. Loki and Hunny became covered in the heavy, thick silt that sucked at them like quicksand.

Loki and Hunny had to move with their family out of their home for a couple of weeks, staying with relatives in Brookhaven. It was here that Loki suddenly became very ill, unable to eat or go to the bathroom. His digestive system shut down and, in excruciating pain, he spent two weeks at the vet while they ran test after test to diagnose his condition. He had an operation and more tests, but still the vets could not tell what was wrong with him. They told Loki's family that there was nothing they could do.

'Take him home for the weekend and say goodbye,' the vets said.

So they took him home, knowing that this would be their last time together. But then, on Saturday, when owner Christine sat munching on some leftover ham, Loki suddenly looked a bit interested. Christine gave him a small piece and he gobbled it down. She gave him another, then another. Finally, after feeding him the whole container of leftovers, Christine picked up the phone and told the vet that Loki would not be coming back.

The vets never could explain

Loki's mystery illness. Some tests suggested it could be copper poisoning, but no one could identify a potential source of the copper. The only other possible explanation the vets could offer was that it was stress.

By February, Loki and Hunny were back with their family in Bexley and Loki's digestive problems had eased. On 22 February 2011, Hunny was inside with Christine and Loki was in the back yard when the big shake hit. Hunny jumped onto Christine's lap, pressing into her as close as she possibly could. Meanwhile, Loki was trying desperately to get inside, smashing his body against the ranch slider again and again.

This time the liquefaction in Bexley was even worse than in September; it was coming straight up through the floors of the house. Outside it was soon waist-deep. Loki was saturated.

The house was so twisted that none of the doors would open, and so Loki was stuck outside while Christine, her two-year-old son Christian and Hunny were trapped inside. Christine opened a window and screamed for help. Eventually two teenage boys heard her cries and were able to help all three of them to squeeze out through the window.

The boys helped drag Hunny and Loki through the thick liquefaction. Hunny, being a little bigger and a lot more energetic than Loki, could manage to jump through it slowly. Loki floundered, trying to swim but mostly having to be dragged reluctantly by his collar.

That night, Loki started throwing up. Christine knew at that stage that they had to get out of Christchurch.

Loki, Hunny and their family spent the next couple of months in Wellington. Loki's stomach condition improved a little, but he also now had a skin problem that had flared up, causing weeping sores all over his body. The vets said it could be an autoimmune disease but it was likely, again, to be simply the result of stress.

Today, Loki has injections every month for his skin condition, and he has a special diet that helps his digestion. His usually fluffy coat is cut short except for a tuft of fur around his head and tail so that his family can see if more sores develop. Unlike Hunny, who still races for the nearest human lap every time there is an aftershock, Loki does not appear to be afraid of the quakes, but he is still in pain and suffers an underlying anxiety that has deeply affected his health.

Loki and Hunny's home in Bexley has been red-zoned, and they are now enjoying living in a brand-new home with a nice big yard that is just a short stroll from the beach.

Bruce

Bruce the white boxer was a very, very energetic one-year-old pup when the 4 September 2010 earthquake hit. His family's house was badly damaged, and they had to move out for three weeks while emergency repairs were completed. They couldn't take Bruce with them, so they tied him to a fence at the house and came back every day to walk and feed him.

The 22 February 2011 quake damaged the house further. Again Bruce's family had to move out, leaving Bruce tied to the fence for another five weeks.

By this time, Bruce had become so stressed and anxious that his family knew he needed to get out of Christchurch. On 25 June 2011, they went to Dogwatch and signed him over to HUHA, which was taking 24 dogs up to Wellington to be re-homed.

Bruce was on a knife-edge, wired all the time while he was in his crate, then completely frantic as soon as he was let out. The HUHA crew gave him lots of Rescue Remedy, a natural stress reliever, to try to ease his anxiety during the big journey up to Wellington.

Once in the capital, HUHA placed Bruce in a foster home, but he lasted just one day, until he ate through the trellis on the fence and was found at the neighbour's house. HUHA knew it was going to be a big challenge to find Bruce a suitable home.

Luckily, Adie was browsing the HUHA website one day and came across Bruce. She immediately thought of her friend, Oscar, who had

lost a white boxer to epilepsy in 2010. Adie hadn't spoken to Oscar in years, but she rang her straight away.

When Oscar had lost her last boxer, she had sworn she would never get another one — and especially not a white one. Boxers are infamous as the 'Peter Pan' of the dog world because they never grow up, and white boxers often have health problems such as blindness, deafness and epilepsy.

But despite her apprehension, as soon as Oscar saw Bruce she knew she had to give him a chance. He was very skinny and couldn't keep food down. HUHA told her that he had very high anxiety levels and lots of behavioural problems.

Oscar was prepared for some naughtiness, but Bruce's behaviour astonished even her. He unstuffed three couches. He escaped and was found kilometres away. He spent hours patrolling the garden perimeter and scaring away anyone who came to the bus stop just outside.

Eventually, Oscar and her partner Emma had to sedate Bruce while they went to work, so that the neighbours wouldn't complain about his behaviour. Emma took him to puppy classes — where he was three times the size of the other, younger pups — so that he could learn some basic obedience skills. They found it hard to be strict on Bruce when he had had such a hard life, so they had a dog trainer come in to set down some ground rules.

All of this care and attention worked, and although Bruce still displays some anxiety — especially when there are earthquakes or loud noises — he is a different dog to the one that boarded the HUHA truck in Christchurch. He can walk on the lead and he doesn't terrorise the neighbours. Oscar and Emma can now let him loose at the dog park and he won't run away. Now he trusts them enough that he will even lie on his back for a good tummy rub.

As soon as Oscar saw Bruce she knew she had to give him a chance.

Guinness

Guinness, a six-year-old Irish wolfhound, is named for his creamy top and big body rather than his drinking abilities. However, on Friday afternoons he used to be found at the historic central city pub, the Carlton Hotel, where he could down a pint of beer in under a minute. After his pint, he would lie on a mat by the front door, where everyone who entered had to step over his not insignificant 80-kilogram body.

Guinness's owner, Sean, describes him as a 'magnet', which could be handy for meeting people at the pub on a Friday night. For the first five years of Guinness's life, he was a familiar sight for those who saw him as he went about his daily routine.

After 22 February 2011, though, when everything in Christchurch was tipped upside down, including routines, Guinness became a source of amusement, distraction and entertainment as he met new people around the city.

Sean and Guinness spent the next 22 days helping residents of the hard-hit eastern suburbs clean up liquefaction and make their homes and roads liveable again. Guinness's main role was to get residents' minds off the quakes; as soon as they saw him, they had something else to talk about. He gave people a break, a reason to laugh — and, for anyone under five years of age, their first-ever dog-ride.

Guinness became such an important character in the clean-up that he was delegated an unofficial mascot for the Student Volunteer Army and

given the honorary title 'Earthquake Dog'. Sean printed the title across the side of his black Jeep so that everyone who saw Guinness with his head sticking out of the back would know who — and what — he was.

Guinness also used his charisma and appearance to help Sean wrangle some free gear to donate to people in the east. Together they distributed more than 800 shovels, 230 wheelbarrows and 1100 bottles of water.

After the earthquake, Guinness and Sean took a road trip to the North Island to thank people for their donations, and along the way visited schools to talk about the value of volunteering. The children had few questions about the earthquakes or volunteering, however; mostly they just wanted to know more about Guinness. At one kindergarten, he gave 18 dog-rides in a single afternoon.

Shortly after the first anniversary of the February quake, Guinness received a medal for being a local hero, part of the annual New Zealander of the Year awards. Sean now has a new job at a construction company, and Guinness spends most days snoozing in the back office and enduring the stares and questions of intrigued clients.

Bentley, Mercedes, Opel & Silvia

When the 22 February 2011 quake struck, Koren's four British bulldogs — Bentley, Mercedes, Opel and Silvia — were all in their crates in the conservatory. It took Koren more than four hours to get home to Bexley from her work in Ferrymead. She started out driving but soon had to resort to walking, sometimes through waist-deep water.

By the time she got home, the bulldogs were chest-deep in liquefaction. They were frozen in their crates like statues with the heavy silt around them, and they were uncharacteristically silent. Their food bowls were floating in a mixture of sewage and water. If Koren had reached them even a half-hour later, the liquefaction would have been over the dogs' heads and they would have drowned.

Koren quickly grabbed the dogs out of their crates and tried to clean off the muddy silt. The house had no running water, so she used wet wipes to do the best she could.

Inside the house, there was not one item of furniture left standing or a single picture left hanging on the walls. Koren thought about the noise that all of the smashing glass and crashing furniture and objects would have made, and how scary this must have been for the dogs.

Koren's van was still stuck in liquefaction, so she and the bulldogs had to wait many hours in the destroyed house before a relative in Rolleston could pick them up in a four-wheel-drive truck. For the

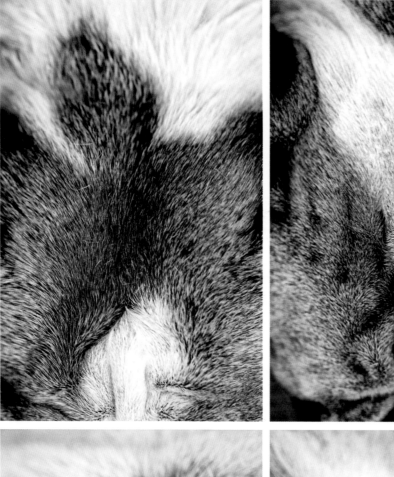
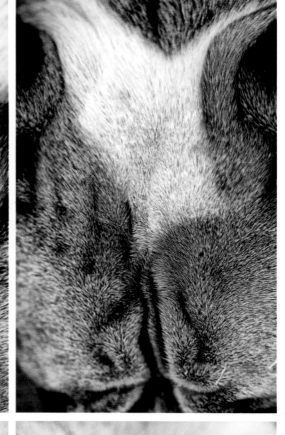

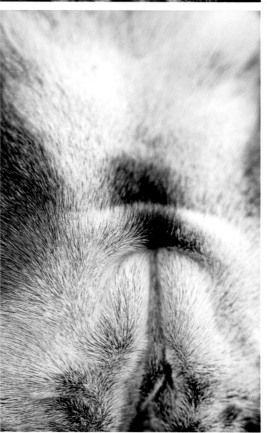

entire night, the usually boisterous dogs remained completely silent, as if in shock following their close brush with death.

All of the dogs were deeply traumatised and soon they began to lose their hair, a condition known as alopecia, which can be caused by stress and anxiety in both humans and dogs. They developed small bald patches and dark, burn-like marks on their skin. Bentley began biting his foot repetitively.

Koren put the dogs on Valium to calm their anxiety, and then as they improved switched to the natural remedy valerian. She bought them all special anti-anxiety shirts, which fitted tightly over their bodies to help comfort them. She covered their skin with soothing medication.

All of these things have helped the bulldogs relax and their hair to regrow, but they still don't like sudden noises such as those made by trucks and especially helicopters, which swooped over their home at low altitude after the September 2010 earthquake. They bark and bark when an aftershock hits, and they hate going in the car. Koren has mostly stopped showing them, as all it takes is for someone to drop a crate loudly beside one of them for their anxiety levels to skyrocket once again.

They were frozen in their crates like statues with the heavy silt around them.

Nemo

Nemo is a 13-year-old Alsatian–beagle mixed breed with a special gift for predicting earthquakes. Every night before a large earthquake strikes, Nemo spends many anxious hours pacing the back garden and barking at the top of his lungs.

Nemo came to live with Steph and her family in Riccarton five years ago. His previous family were going to have him put down, but a last-ditch effort on TradeMe found Nemo a great new home with a gentle and loving playmate, Lucy, a bull mastiff–boxer cross.

Finding Nemo was a momentous event in all of their lives. Lucy in particular was happy to have a new friend for her adventures. One day the pair jumped the fence and followed the usual route towards their favourite beach. Strangers picked them up almost five kilometres from home.

Nemo's favourite pastime is playing with a ball. Several years ago he almost had to give up this hobby when he developed arthritis in his toe. The vets said either he had to stop chasing balls or they would have to amputate the toe. There was no deliberation. The toe came off and Nemo didn't even notice it was gone. That was Nemo's second lucky break.

The night before the 4 September 2010 quake, Nemo spent the entire night running out into the back garden and barking incessantly.

The behaviour was so unlike him that Steph checked the yard several times to see what was out there. Only Nemo could see — or feel — the impending doom. After the quake, Nemo was quiet but anxious.

There were no more barking episodes until the night before the 22 February 2011 quake, when he once again spent all night barking. On 12 June 2011, when he barked all night again, Steph knew that another big quake was imminent. They cancelled all plans the next day and stayed at home, waiting for the shakes that, sure enough, rocked the city once more.

Now that aftershocks are infrequent, Nemo is less anxious, but the earthquakes have aged him. His muzzle is speckled with grey and his legs shake. He spends most of his time outside, listening intently and barking when trucks rumble by.

In November, Lucy and Nemo had to move to a kennel for six weeks while their house was being repaired. They didn't mind the holiday, especially since they got to visit their family on Sundays and they could roam their now empty house, sniffing in newly exposed nooks and crannies. Also, as an added bonus, the kennel owners let them bark as loudly as they could — not like at home, where they were scolded if they made a racket. By the time they got home, both Nemo and Lucy had lost their voices.

Grace

Animal Control found Grace walking the streets of Ashburton when she was just eight weeks old. The bull mastiff's owner never came to claim her, and so Trisha and Brad rescued her from the pound and planned to find her a good home through their K9 Rescue and Rehoming organisation.

These plans were thwarted when the day after Grace came to live with them, she developed the potentially deadly dog disease parvovirus.

Trisha and Brad knew how much it would cost to have Grace treated, but they had already grown to love her and were determined to save her, no matter what the cost. Grace stayed at the vet clinic for five days in isolation. Miraculously, she pulled through and proceeded to grow into the nicest, most subdued dog her owners had ever known.

When the 4 September 2010 quake struck, Grace was asleep in her crate under the stairwell in their Wainoni home. A row of hand-painted wine glasses that had just been made for Trisha and Brad's wedding smashed into a million pieces in front of her. The water in the fish tank not far from her bed sloshed over the sides until it was almost empty.

As soon as the shaking stopped, Trisha, Brad and their children ran downstairs and grabbed Grace out of her crate. They all huddled under the table in the living room until it was finally light outside.

Grace became increasingly anxious after the quake and spent most of her time outside in the yard, where the aftershocks weren't quite so scary. On Boxing Day 2010 the yard didn't prove to be the safest place, however, when a big aftershock sent a 6 tonne tree crashing through the side of the house, taking out part of the shed and fence. Grace and the other dogs ran inside for comfort.

After this, Grace's personality completely changed. She became terrified of anything that made noises or moved. She started trying to attack the microwave when it beeped and the phone when it rang. She became scared of towels blowing on the line, kids on scooters, flags flapping in the wind, towels on the beach, sprinklers and the hose.

The hardest change of all, though, was Grace's new aggressiveness towards other dogs. Trisha and Brad had five other dogs and they regularly fostered many others waiting for new homes. At one stage, they were caring for 25 dogs! Grace had to be kept separate from all of them, and could no longer visit the dog park or run free on the beach.

Trisha and Brad thought Grace's social life with other dogs was over, but then Tully, a six-week-old brindle bull mastiff from Blenheim, came along. Tully, who had a severe hernia in her belly button, is now Grace's best friend, and they both cry every time they have to be apart.

Grace's personality completely changed. She became terrified of anything that made noises or moved.

Angel

Angel lives with Robynne and an odd assortment of other animals. In addition to three other harlequin Great Danes — her sisters, Faith and Pagan, and her mum Rokky — Angel also lives with 13 Sphynx (hairless) cats and seven cats of various other breeds. It is odd to watch a small hairless cat and one of the tallest dogs in the world playing together, but all of the animals seem to peacefully coexist.

Angel is six years old and weighs 62 kilograms. Her favourite pastimes are walking in Burwood Forest and driving in the van with Robynne, but it will come as no surprise that eating is also high on her priority list. In the morning, breakfast is a dozen dog biscuits and a big slice of dog roll, and in the evening, dinner consists of four cups of dried kibble. If Angel is lucky, Robynne might share an ice cream or other treat with her for dessert.

Through the 4 September 2010 and 22 February 2011 earthquakes and the many aftershocks, Angel and her other animal housemates all appeared to be relatively calm and unaffected. During the big shakes, Angel would jump up and watch the lights swinging from the ceiling, but she soon relaxed when she saw that Robynne was not afraid. Little did Robynne know that the thousands of aftershocks were silently taking their toll on Angel.

When a large aftershock hit on 23 December 2011, Angel and the other animals seemed to react normally. However, later that evening, Angel went outside to the

toilet and didn't come back. Robynne went to look for her and found her standing in a corner of the garden with her head down. Her stomach was hard and distended. Robynne immediately knew that Angel had a condition called bloat, which she had seen before in other dogs. She knew from experience that bloat was life-threatening and that she had to get Angel to a vet immediately.

Gastric dilatation-volvulus, or bloat as it is commonly called, is a condition to which deep-chested dogs such as Great Danes are particularly susceptible. It occurs when the dog's stomach overfills with gas and twists on itself, causing terrible damage and often death within a very short time. The experts are not certain about what causes bloat, but stress is definitely a factor. Studies have shown that dogs that

are fearful have an increased risk of developing bloat.

Although it was late at night, Robynne immediately rushed Angel to the emergency vet. As soon as they arrived, the vet stabilised Angel and began to operate. The dangerous surgery involved cutting open Angel's chest, untwisting her stomach and then tacking the stomach to the abdomen wall so that it wouldn't twist again.

The $1400 operation was success-ful, and Angel was able to go home the next day. From Angel's perspective, the worst consequence was decreased rations for a while, but before long she was back to her normal routine of playing with hairless cats and lounging on the couch. Robynne is very relieved that her beloved Angel is not another quake statistic.

Jessie

Just after the 13 June 2011 earthquake struck, Animal Control found three-month-old Jessie aimlessly wandering the streets of Riccarton. They brought the collie cross to the pound, where she stayed for two long weeks with no contact from her original owner or anyone else willing to adopt her. After 14 days, twice the normal time allowed, Jessie's time was up.

But on that day, for some completely inexplicable reason, Yolanda stopped by the pound on her way home from work. Working as a dog trainer and walker, Yolanda usually avoided the pound because she found it depressing, but on this day she felt peculiarly drawn to visit.

Yolanda was interested in one of the pound dogs, but someone else had already asked to adopt him. She turned to leave when she saw a black-and-white puppy jumping up and down and making a bit of a stir. Noticing the pup had caught Yolanda's eye, a dog control officer asked if she would like to take her for a walk. He thrust the lead into Yolanda's hand and said, 'Go on, take her outside!'

Yolanda took the lead and led the pup around the pound yard. The pup looked up at her with imploring eyes that said, 'Look no further — you've found me', and Yolanda knew she was hooked. She rang her partner, Dennis, and told him to come to the pound. Together they saw that this wee girl with her busy nature would suit them wonderfully. Given how Yolanda had

found her, it felt like the pup was just meant to be with them.

From here on, Jessie's life was to become wonderfully exciting. In some ways, Christchurch had become more dog-friendly than it had ever been, because the red zone had little traffic and fewer people. Jessie regularly walked around the red zone with Dennis and Yolanda. Jessie was one of the first dogs to run in Latimer Square when the cordon was reduced. She was also one of the first pet dogs to walk through the Re:Start container mall — and the first to be politely asked to leave, as city bylaws mean dogs aren't allowed there.

Having never known a world without aftershocks, Jessie wasn't afraid of quakes, but cars and other traffic frightened her greatly. Yolanda and Dennis used their walks around the city to get her used to cars, big machinery and the many noisy trucks that rumbled in and out of the central city. She is now as comfortable on busy city streets as she is on the quiet beach near her home.

It felt like the pup was just meant to be with them.

Cilla

Cilla, a two-year-old Boston terrier, was born into a prestigious line just before the February 2011 earthquake. Both Cilla's mum and dad were New Zealand show champions, and the 'Fantastic Five', as breeder Val called the puppies, were all named after Beatles songs. Cilla's kennel name became 'Bostonite Love of the Loved', a song that Paul McCartney wrote for fellow performer Cilla Black.

Cilla slept right through the big February earthquake, but as she grew older, the many aftershocks began to wear on her nerves. The 13 June 2011 aftershocks were the last straw: she began losing weight, her hair fell out and her ears lay flat against her head.

Val had hoped to keep Cilla for showing and breeding, but she soon realised that the little dog needed to get out of Christchurch. As fate would have it, the very day that Val decided to find Cilla a new home, she got a phone call. Karleen and her partner Adie were trying to find a Boston terrier as a playmate for their French bulldog, Burton, who was definitely not your typical low-energy, placid Frenchie. Cilla would fit in perfectly, as an older dog would be better able to handle Burton's intensity.

Val's interview with Cilla's potential new family was stricter than any job interview, but afterwards she was confident that Cilla would love her beautiful new home in the countryside north of Auckland. In July 2012, Val said a tearful goodbye and put Cilla on a plane for her new home.

The first day that Cilla was with Adie and Karleen, she romped through the paddocks, eating horse and sheep poo and splashing through mud puddles. Karleen and Adie knew then that the little show dog would adapt just fine to life in the country.

At first Cilla was terrified of Burton, and would run and hide in her crate every time he tried to play with her. But slowly she became more and more confident, and soon she started chewing his face, the only part of him she could grab onto. Before long, Burton and Cilla were the best of friends.

Sadly, not long after Cilla arrived, Burton was hit by a courier van and died. Cilla was also hit by the van, and had some cuts and grazes to recover from, but the worst pain was losing her mate. She walked around the house and property looking for Burton for a couple of weeks, jumping up to investigate every little noise, hoping it might be him.

Adie and Karleen knew they needed to find her a new friend, as she had never been without other dogs to keep her company. They soon found another Frenchie, Oakley, who would become Cilla's new partner in crime. They now spend their days together, tromping through the muddy pond, bobbing for balls in the swimming pool and chasing each other in loops around the chickens and turkeys in the front yard.

The little show dog would adapt just fine to life in the country.

Easy

Easy, the 'old fella' as handler Brenda calls him, is a 10-year-old curly-coated retriever–border collie cross and the most experienced of Brenda's three USAR dogs (see also pages 14 and 274). He is fast, yet very methodical, so on 22 February 2011, Brenda chose him to search The Press building, where it was thought that four people were trapped.

To reach the top of the old building, Brenda and Easy had to go up the stairwell of the new Press building in complete darkness, climb a ladder and then cross the space between the two buildings. Easy confirmed the location of the four people, three of whom were rescued alive, and also confirmed that no other people were trapped there.

On their way out of The Press building, Brenda and Easy had to navigate their way out of the pitch-black building, with no light except a headlamp. Then the batteries in the headlamp died. They had no choice but to try to feel their way out through the darkness, going down several floors too far then back up a couple of levels to find the way out. It was one of the most anxious moments of the day.

Once out on the street, the pair became disoriented amid the pandemonium. A policewoman stopped Brenda and asked for Easy to search a row of cars that had been crushed by falling masonry. As he searched, Easy whined and whimpered, staring intently at several of the cars.

Like other New Zealand USAR

dogs, Easy can distinguish people who are alive from dead bodies. While he barks frantically wherever he thinks there is a 'scent pool' from a live body, he is trained to not react when finding a corpse. Dogs that are trained to not respond to dead bodies will react in different ways, but Easy whines and looks fixedly at the place where the scent is coming from.

Towards the end of their massive, 30-hour shift, Easy got a small cut on his paw. USAR dogs don't wear boots because they need their paws exposed so that they can feel and grip uneven surfaces. Given the amount of glass, wire and sharp rubble he

had worked over and through, Brenda says it was amazing that neither he nor any of the other dogs were seriously hurt.

Easy and Brenda finally took their first break after working for almost a day and a half straight. They rested for just two hours on the floor of another handler's house before resuming their searches.

Once teams from the North Island and overseas began arriving, they could shorten their shifts to 12 hours at a time, a routine Easy, Brenda and her two other dogs kept up for the next 30 days, together conducting over 40 searches.

Easy and Brenda finally took their first break after working for almost a day and a half straight.

Tara & Adam

Prior to the 4 September 2010 quake, Dan's one-year-old collie, Adam, had severe separation anxiety disorder and would chew anything available when Dan left him. He chewed CDs, the stairwell, the carpet and an entire couch. Nothing Dan did seemed to stop Adam's behaviour, so he asked a dog trainer for advice.

After observing Dan with Adam and his other collie, Tara, the trainer told Dan that, while he was physically looking after the dogs very well, he was treating them like children instead of dogs.

The trainer told Dan to feed himself first, then 10-year-old Tara, and finally Adam. He was told to keep Tara and Adam behind him on their leads when walking, and to always go first through the doorway and then let the dogs follow. Most importantly, Tara and Adam were absolutely not to sleep on Dan's bed or even in his room. As they had been sleeping on Dan's bed all their lives, this was going to be a hard change for them — and even more so for Dan.

When Dan went to bed on 3 September, feeling guilty and mean, he shut Adam outside his room. He figured that since Tara had been well-behaved she could stay in the bedroom with him.

Shortly after 4 a.m., the house began to shake and Dan clung to Tara for the full 40 seconds of the quake. He was so confused and shocked that he didn't think to call for Adam, but as soon as

the shaking stopped, Dan opened the bedroom door and shouted for the dog. Adam didn't come. It was pitch black and there was no power, so Dan tried to feel his way to the stairs, but a bookcase was blocking his way. He was starting to have visions of Adam being squashed underneath a large item of furniture. Of all the nights for this to happen, he thought. Adam had always been with him in his room at night, never shut out on his own.

After some minutes of Dan calling desperately for him, Adam suddenly brushed past his leg. Dan had no idea where he had come from, but all that mattered was that he was alive and apparently unharmed. Dan was so glad that he hadn't called the dog upstairs while the quake was happening, as the bookcase might have fallen on him when he was coming up the stairs.

From that night on, Dan has been the one with separation anxiety. He just can't leave Adam and Tara at home alone in case another earthquake hits. Adam now sleeps in Dan's room again and he no longer chews the furniture.

Harry

Harry, a Dobermann–Rottweiler–huntaway cross, was just two months old when the 22 February 2011 quake hit. He was part of an unwanted litter, rescued by Paw Justice and brought to Dogwatch.

Dogwatch had no room for him, as the quakes meant they already had twice as many dogs as they could normally house, many in makeshift crates in the garden. However, they found a place for him on the HUHA truck that was taking stressed and abandoned dogs north to Wellington to be re-homed.

When the HUHA truck arrived in Wellington, Harry was the last Christchurch puppy to be taken home, but he was soon to go from rags to riches. Harry became Bavani and Graham's first dog, and they showered him with a soft bed, warm blankets,

fun toys and yummy food. They had a special dog trainer visit to make sure they had everything just the way a dog like Harry would want it.

Bavani and Graham also took Harry to the vet to be neutered and checked over. The vet gave him a clean bill of health, apart from a small lump on his ear. He told them it was nothing to worry about but to bring Harry back if it changed.

When Harry first came to live with Bavani and Graham, he was nervous of both other dogs and people, and he didn't like anyone to

touch him. But with such a loving family, he soon came out of his shell and learned to trust humans again. Bavani and Graham also began taking him for sleepovers at a kennel in Raglan where he could socialise with doggie friends.

On Christmas Day 2011, Bavani was giving Harry a good scratch around the ears when she noticed that the lump on his ear had turned into a scab. Four days later, it turned into a bubble and then burst. A week later, they were told Harry had skin cancer.

Harry was operated on in January 2012; luckily the cancer hadn't spread but his ear had to be removed. When they brought him home, Bavani and Graham moved their bed into the lounge and slept with their eyes half-open to make sure Harry didn't sleep on his bad ear. He wouldn't wear his Elizabethan collar, so they had to keep a close eye on him to make sure he didn't scratch his wound. They alternated taking time off work so that there was always someone with him.

Harry finally got his energy back about seven weeks after the operation, and he now doesn't seem to mind — or even notice — that his ear is missing. Now that Harry has recovered, Bavani and Graham have decided to move to the Gold Coast and will take Harry with them. His flight will cost $1300, plus the medical tests needed to get him through immigration. Bavani has researched the best flight route with shortest stopovers, and they will be able to pick him up just two hours after he lands.

Bailey

Bailey, a border collie–Alsatian cross, came from the pound to live with Michelle and her family when he was two years old. Now 13, Bailey's muzzle may be slightly grey, but when there's a ball in his mouth, he still feels like he's a pup.

Bailey was raised as an outside dog, but when the 4 September 2010 quake hit, the inside lifestyle was instantly much more appealing. It took many months for him to even go back into his kennel, where he had been at the time of that first big shake.

On 22 February 2011, Bailey was at home alone when the big quake struck. Michelle was in town but luckily was able to get home quite quickly. She was very relieved to find Bailey still in the yard when she returned, as they usually kept the gate open. Bailey was not a wanderer, and he often dug himself a nest in the dirt just inside the fence, where he could keep an eye on everyone coming and going.

Knowing that Bailey and the rest of the family were safe, Michelle's mind turned to practical matters. She realised they were out of basics like milk and bread and, unsure exactly how the quake might affect supplies, she drove to the dairy two blocks away to stock up just in case.

She was gone just five minutes, but when she returned Bailey was gone. The family took to the streets, calling

his name. Michelle kicked herself for not closing the gate, but Bailey had never gone wandering before.

Michelle tried ringing the pound but she couldn't get through. She heard on the radio that local, temporary pounds had been set up, where animals were being kept for 24 hours before they were taken to the main service centres. Michelle visited and found lots of scared animals — but no sign of Bailey.

They kept up the search for five anxious days, putting out food each night, searching and calling endlessly and visiting the local temporary pound every day. Finally, on day five, they got a phone call from the pound. Bailey was at a neighbour's house, just around the corner. He must have followed Michelle to the dairy and lost his way. All that time he had been just metres away.

The neighbour had been trying to ring the pound, but with many phone lines down and the pound so busy, it took her five days to get through. She knew someone would be desperately searching for Bailey, but at the same time, deep down she was also quite happy to have the dog with her. Her son had moved out just two days before and it was lonely being on her own. She later told Michelle that Bailey was an 'angel' and she didn't know what she would have done if he hadn't been there. Every time there was an aftershock, they would huddle together, shaking in each other's arms.

Bailey was not entirely unhappy with the situation either. His new caretaker had pampered him, buying him toys and a new brush and taking him everywhere with her. But still he missed home. When Michelle finally showed up, Bailey jumped in the car and never looked back.

Blondie

On 22 February 2011, Blondie was inside her home with owner Sandy and her other Chinese crested dogs. As soon as the shaking had subsided enough so that they could move, Blondie and the other dogs ran outside as fast as they could.

The dogs scattered, and Blondie ran straight into a small gap between a wall and the garden shed. By the time Sandy got outside to try to calm the dogs, Blondie was wedged tightly into the small crevice. She was too far in for Sandy to reach her.

Sandy took the other dogs inside to settle them down and to think about how she might pry Blondie out of her awkward position. For over an hour, Sandy paced and wondered how she could get Blondie out of her predicament. She had finally decided that the only way to get her out was to pull the shed to bits when suddenly Blondie crept in through the back door. Sandy guessed that her muscles must have relaxed enough to allow her to wriggle and squeeze her own way back out.

Before this experience, Blondie had had a typical personality for a Chinese crested dog: she was very confident and outgoing and enjoyed being with people. However, after the big quake, Blondie's temperament changed. She became very timid and was defensive when anyone came close to her. She was worst with strangers, but

she would even bark frantically at people she knew until they sat down and she got used to them being close.

Her behaviour became unpredictable. While she was just fine some days, on other days she was completely on edge. She began sleeping under her hammock bed rather than on it, while most of the other dogs started to sleep outside, even in the middle of winter.

Blondie had once been a New Zealand show champion, but after February 2011, her nervous disposition made that difficult. At Blondie's last show, Sandy put her on the table to be examined and she bolted before the judge could touch her. Sandy hasn't put her back in the ring since, too concerned by how stressful shows must be for her.

As the tremors become less frequent, Blondie's nerves seem to be settling, but sometimes she will get a wild, terrified look in her eyes. On these occasions, Sandy worries about what the dog might do. She doesn't know what triggers these episodes, but Blondie always comes out of it eventually. She does still enjoy going to shows with Sandy and the other dogs, and Sandy hopes that one day Blondie might recover enough to enter the ring again.

Lewis

Lewis is a four-year-old Labrador–border collie cross with an abundance of energy and a slight mischievous streak. He is a strong and focused dog when he is working, but off-duty he has been known to steal the odd defrosting steak.

Craig got Lewis from the pound when he was eight months old and set about training him as a USAR dog straight away. He became certified to participate in real search-and-rescue operations just a year later in 2010. His usual searching toy is a towel wrapped in duct tape, which he gets as a reward only when he is practising searches. Lewis loves the towel so much that when he gets it, he runs away with it and staunchly refuses to give it back.

On 22 February 2011, Craig was stuck in Western Australia due to a cyclone, far away from his wife and Lewis, who were at home in Mt Pleasant when the quake hit. It was two days before Craig could get back to Christchurch. He arrived on the Thursday morning and spent the day resting up before he and Lewis headed out on their first night shift in the CBD.

Most of their time in the city was spent 'clearing' areas — confirming there were no live victims trapped in fallen buildings. The other USAR handlers were grateful to have Craig and Lewis fresh on the scene,

relieving the pressure on the small team that had been working such long hours since the quake hit.

After several days had passed, Craig and the other handlers had to find a way to keep the dogs motivated because the dogs were working long hours. They set up small search exercises in the empty city streets. One handler would run away and hide, then the dogs would be set loose to go and find him or her, receiving their search toys when they made the find.

Lewis and Craig worked 12-hour night shifts for the first three days, and then 12-hour day shifts for another 10 days after that. Lewis enjoyed the work, and he continued to search and clear areas with determination and drive. He was calm and seemingly unaffected by the aftershocks.

Although Lewis had no problems with the earthquakes themselves, things at home were a bit more problematic. Their home was uninhabitable after 22 February, so Craig, his wife and Lewis moved in with friends for a while, then went to the North Island for a stint. All of the moving around unsettled Lewis. He became stressed, and as an odd side-effect, he would pee for an unusually long time. The Veterinary Emergency Response Team (VERT) that had looked after the dogs during the search operation cleared him of any long-term effects, and the behaviour soon went away when they settled in to their new home in Hanmer Springs.

After the quakes, Lewis and Craig and another USAR dog, Cairo, and his handler, Janelle (see page 128), visited the Dallington Boy Scout group to do a presentation about their work. Both Lewis and Cairo received a Scout badge for 'being prepared'.

Lewis enjoyed the work, and he continued to search and clear areas with determination and drive.

Piper

Unlike many other dogs, who suffered severe anxiety after being home alone during the 22 February 2011 quake, being inside may well have saved the lives of Piper and her mother Lexi. The back yard, where they could have been, was buried under half a metre of liquefaction.

Owner Jill believes the Dalmatians probably would have drowned in the sinkholes that emerged around the yard, swallowing hoses and other objects — some of which resurfaced months later.

Jill was at work in the city during the quake, and it took her the best part of four hours to drive home to New Brighton. She had to park a block away from her house because the road in front of her house had suffered major damage, and the liquefaction was ankle-deep. After she walked home, a kind neighbour offered to go inside with her, saying she shouldn't have to face it alone.

Jill managed to get into the house, although the concrete paths were at odd angles and the garage door couldn't be opened. Liquefaction had run throughout the house. However, Piper and Lexi were unharmed and were very pleased to see her. She collected a few things for herself and the dogs and walked with them back to the car through the thick silt.

They moved in with Jill's mother, Beryl, and her three Dalmatians: Evie, James and Annie. There was

no water or power, so Jill went with neighbours each day to fill containers of water from a collection point.

Once the liquefaction in the park drained away, Jill and Beryl took the dogs for a walk. Annie was ambling along, sniffing and re-acquainting herself with familiar smells, when she suddenly disappeared down a deep sinkhole. Jill had to clamber down and hoist out the surprised but unhurt dog.

Perhaps because Lexi, Evie, James and Annie were older than Piper, the quakes didn't seem to affect them. But as the aftershocks continued, Jill noticed that Piper became increasingly nervous. Whenever a tremor hit, she would jump up, whine and look for comfort.

When the 23 December 2011 quake hit, Piper was so distraught that she kept clawing Jill's legs, trying to climb onto her lap. Jill's legs were covered in bruises afterwards.

Sadly, old age caught up with 13-year-old James, then 15-year-old Evie. Months later, when 13-year-old Annie and 15-year-old Lexi were also laid to rest, Jill wondered how Piper would cope, being on her own for the first time in her life. Piper still notices every tremor, and as Jill and Beryl form her pack now, she voices strong disapproval if they leave the house without her.

Meg

Meg is a gentle, 13-year-old golden retriever whose favourite activities are playing with her soft toys and unwrapping presents. Every Christmas and birthday she gets a new toy to add to her collection, and her bed is overflowing with a rainbow assortment of cuddly creatures, from pigs and teddy bears to snowmen and dinosaurs.

Her own bed is so full that sometimes she sneaks into the humans' bed with her owner Tracey, when Tracey's husband Peter is on night shift. She listens carefully for Peter to come home so she can quietly slink off, leaving a nice warm patch for Peter to crawl into. Only once has she fallen into such a deep sleep that Peter has caught her comfortably tucked in beside Tracey with her head on his pillow.

Meg is happiest when she is close to her family, so when the 4 September 2010 quake hit and she was by herself in the kitchen, all she wanted to do was find Tracey and Peter. Above the horrendous noise, she must have heard Tracey screaming at the other end of the hall. She would have seen Peter desperately grabbing kids and shoving them under door frames. In her desperation, Meg somehow managed to open the heavy sliding door that trapped her in the kitchen. Shaking with fear, she dodged flying objects to take cover with the rest of the family under a door frame.

During the 22 February 2011 earthquake, Meg was again at home,

this time with Peter and his son Alex. Once again Peter and Alex crawled into a door frame, and Meg quickly followed while the house's contents exploded around them.

With this experience behind her, Meg learned that each time an aftershock hit, the best option was to take refuge under a door frame. Now, even if it is only a very small shake, Meg runs for a doorway and stares at Tracey and Peter expectantly, wondering why they aren't running to join her.

Meg was home alone when the first June 2011 quake hit, but Tracey and her parents made it home quickly to reassure Meg and clear up yet another mess of broken glass and fallen furniture. They went outside to investigate if the roof and brick walls had been damaged further, with Meg following dutifully by Tracey's side. A second, bigger quake hit while they were in the yard. Tracey and her parents fell to their knees and huddled together. Meg lay down with them, content just to be with them since there were no door frames in sight.

Superficially, Meg's house appears to have held up well in the quakes, with only a few cracks and doors that won't shut. However, underneath this façade is hidden major structural damage. Their house is earmarked to be demolished soon, and Meg and her family will join the queue of families searching for dog-friendly rental accommodation until their new house can be built.

MyLo

MyLo is a seven-year-old Labrador—Staffie cross that came to Christchurch just months before the 22 February 2011 quake. Animal Control had found her wandering the streets of Ashburton in November 2010 and took her to the pound. She was scheduled to be put down when Marie found out about her from K9 Rescue and Rehoming. She drove to Ashburton to meet her.

When she opened up the cage, MyLo walked to her and, staring her in the eyes, sat down right in front of her. Marie burst into tears and knew it was meant to be.

Perhaps sensing her good fortune in being rescued, MyLo was a model pet. She loved kids, didn't jump on the furniture and didn't care about cats. She loved to ride in the car, and Marie wouldn't go anywhere without her.

On 22 February 2011, Marie and MyLo had just emerged from Bottle Lake Forest when the big quake struck. As soon as the shaking subsided, they quickly jumped in the car, as Marie wanted to get to her grandson at school on Moorhouse Avenue. They managed to get across several bridges before they were closed, but at Bealey Avenue an army cordon stopped them from going any further.

Marie dumped the car and she and MyLo headed the rest of the way on foot. They comforted each other through the long three and a half hours it took them to finally make it to the school. Recalling the many horrors they saw that day, Marie says she wouldn't have made it without MyLo.

When they finally made it back to their house in Parklands, just south of Bottle Lake, about 6 p.m., they found their rented house was damaged but still liveable. But several weeks later, Marie lost her job because her position was no longer available after the quake. Then, to make matters worse, her husband Dean was laid off too, because his company's premises had been destroyed.

With no income, Marie and Dean could no longer afford their rent. Neither of them could find a job in Christchurch, and so when Dean was offered another job in Auckland, they felt they had no choice but to move. They didn't know if they would ever be able to come back to Christchurch.

Given their situation, they decided — despite their huge regret and sadness — that it would be better for MyLo to find another home. Marie rang K9 Rescue and asked for their help in saving MyLo one more time. It broke Marie's heart, but she knew it had to be done for MyLo's sake.

When the ad for MyLo appeared on the K9 Rescue website, it caught Amy's eye because it said that MyLo followed her owner everywhere. Amy was looking for a companion to always be with her, so it sounded like a good fit.

At first, MyLo was very timid; for a few weeks she cowered in a corner, flinching at any sudden movement or noise. However, she soon settled in to her new home in the country, and she now goes everywhere with Amy and Jeremy. She especially loves going to work with Amy at Bunny Lodge kennels, where she can socialise with all the other animals. She still loves riding in the car, and relishes her many holidays camping and boating around the South Island.

Rocky

Rocky is a 10-year-old Staffie-terrier cross who came to live with Jennie and Matavai six years ago when her previous owner moved overseas. Rocky's favourite things are treats and swimming in the sea. She is a sensitive soul who has always been timid around strangers.

On 4 September 2010, Rocky was home with Jennie, who was seven months pregnant, and her two-year-old son, Matai. When Jennie heard the rumbling, she leapt out of bed, grabbed Matai from his cot and huddled under a door frame. It wasn't until the power went out and the house alarm started blaring that Rocky ran to them. They all stayed under the doorway until the shaking stopped. Rocky was hyperventilating and trembling with fear.

After the quake, Rocky's personality changed. She would run away almost every day. If she was locked inside the house, she would try to escape by chewing through doors and window frames, and if she was left outside in the garden, she would jump the 1.8 metre fence. If she was tied up, she would become incredibly distressed. She paced back and forth and wouldn't eat or sleep.

For five months after the September quake, Jennie took Rocky with her everywhere she could, but it was difficult with a newborn and a two-year-old to look after. Jennie's parents minded Rocky from

time to time, but her behaviour was unmanageable.

The vet prescribed tranquillisers for Rocky, but even then the continuing aftershocks would make her hyperventilate for long periods of time. Nothing seemed to comfort her.

When the 22 February 2011 earthquake hit, Rocky spent 24 hours pacing and hyperventilating. Jennie and Matavai knew they had to do something for her. They decided to ask friends who lived in Dunedin if they could temporarily give her a home. They agreed, and Rocky moved south for the next 18 months.

Although Rocky missed her family, she was happy to be away from the quakes and settled into her new life in Dunedin. She had only the odd moment of panic — like when the smoke alarm went off, reminding her of the aftermath of the September 2010 quake, and she leapt out a second-storey window.

Rocky returned to her home in Christchurch in September 2012, two years after the first big quake. She still suffers from separation anxiety and doesn't like being left alone for more than a few hours at a time. However, she is happy to be home and is slowly settling into her old routine.

Stig

Stig became an operational New Zealand Land Search and Rescue (LandSAR) dog in 2003, when he was just three years old. Over the past 10 years, the German short-haired pointer has worked with Dave on more than 70 search-and-rescue operations.

Among their achievements are saving a hunter's life in the mountains near Mt Hutt, and receiving an award at Parliament for finding the body of Irina Yun, who had been missing for over a year, in the Dart River. Through years of living and working together so closely, Dave and Stig have developed a very strong bond.

Stig was at home in Sumner with Dave's other dogs, Enzo and Lexi, when the 22 February 2011 earthquake struck. Dave was in Lyttelton, and knew immediately that search dogs would be needed. To get home to Stig,

he first tried to go over Evans Pass. As he was driving by the Timeball Station, an aftershock hit and a wall collapsed onto the road in front of him. The Lyttelton tunnel was closed too, so his only option was to take the circuitous route via Governors Bay and over Dyers Pass. The roads were all solid with traffic, and it took him hours to get home.

When he finally got to Sumner, Dave quickly picked up Stig and they then battled more traffic to get to the main Civil Defence headquarters in the city. Eventually, they were

deployed with a police team to a city church that had collapsed. Stig searched the area systematically, working into the wind so that he could smell as acutely as possible. Before long he started digging and barking. Later that night, searchers located three bodies at that very spot.

Stig and Dave got home very late that night. Six other families were camping in their lounge, as their house had gas and water for cooking. One family had lost their house and another had been red-stickered due to rock-fall danger. One couple stayed with them for a month until they could find another place to live.

The next day, Stig and Dave were deployed with other LandSAR teams to search the hills around Sumner and Redcliffs. Many cars had been abandoned, and Dave recorded the licence-plate numbers so that he could find out if any of the drivers were still missing. They cleared a huge area of the Port Hills over the next few days.

Stig continues his search and rescue work, but his 10 years of service have taken a toll on his body. His spine has degenerated and he may have to retire this year. Dave is hoping he can continue to do water searches in his retirement.

Maggie

One night in June 2011, Rob and Sarndra were watching Campbell Live when they heard for the first time about Dogwatch, a sanctuary for pound dogs on death row, which had been inundated with dogs after the February quake.

Because there were so many dogs and so few homes in Canterbury that could take them, Dogwatch was working with an organisation called HUHA to take 24 dogs up to Wellington to be re-homed.

This piqued their interest, so Rob popped down to Dogwatch the next day to check out the dogs there. None of them seemed to be just what he was looking for, but Dogwatch suggested that he go around the corner to the council pound. As soon as he walked in, a huntaway–collie cross caught his eye.

The pound wouldn't disclose any information about where the dog had been abandoned, except that she had been left on a deserted property, tied to a fence. She had a microchip, but it held no information. They thought she was about one year old.

As the dog was a new arrival, Rob couldn't take her yet in case she was claimed. He left his name and phone number and the pound said they would be in contact in a couple of weeks.

One Tuesday lunchtime a few weeks later, Rob got a phone call. 'Do you want this dog? If not, she's

being put down this afternoon.'

Rob called Sarndra, who decided they had better grab the children and meet at the pound after work. Sarndra and the kids took the dog for a walk and unanimously declared her 'delightful'. But, not wanting to rush into anything, they decided to go home and sleep on it. The pound officer agreed to wait until lunchtime the next day.

A family meeting that night was largely dominated by the children's anxious pleas and promises to walk, feed and pick up poo. They were adamant that they had to save the dog and couldn't let her die. So it was agreed: this earthquake orphan would have a new home, and they would call her Maggie, short for magnitude.

Rob and Sarndra picked up Maggie the next afternoon, brought her home, bathed her and took her to the vet. She is now one of the family. She spends happy days chasing balls and swimming in the river, with only thunderstorms and the occasional aftershock to worry about.

Blaze

Blaze is a five-year-old mixed breed from the SPCA. She's named for the white blaze up her nose, as well as her 'quick as a blaze' reactions. When earthquakes hit, Blaze is true to her name and hurtles under the bed, where she remains for as long as possible.

Owner Angela, who at the time of the 22 February 2011 earthquake worked at a doggie daycare, describes Blaze as 'more human than dog'. She has four large crates of toys that line the lounge wall. Blaze's favourite toy is a simple cloth star, which she likes nibbling at the seams.

Blaze and her family live in Aranui, a suburb hard-hit by liquefaction after the 22 February 2011 earthquake. A couple of months after that quake, Angela took Blaze in for routine surgery to remove a small lump on her thigh, and to her surprise found that Blaze had a high temperature. In every other way Blaze appeared to feel fine, but Angela asked for a blood test to find out what was going on.

The results from the blood work astounded the vet and Angela. Blaze's liver enzyme levels were so high they couldn't even be measured. More blood tests and then an ultrasound confirmed that Blaze had serious liver damage. In May, Blaze had her first biopsy, which showed she had virtually no normal liver tissue left.

The vet said it was terminal and gave Blaze just six months to live.

This was unbelievable news, since Blaze showed no other signs of being sick besides a high temperature. Her energetic and loving personality still shone through.

The vet, Steve Gray, was unable to explain what had caused Blaze's sickness, but he suspected that a toxin was attacking her liver. The symptoms were very similar to copper poisoning. Despite reassurances that her condition had nothing to do with the earthquakes, Angela had to wonder about the liquefaction and dust surrounding her house. She thought of the big grey footprints Blaze tracked into the house after the February quake.

Angela resolved to do everything she could to try to save Blaze. Blaze stayed at the vet clinic for a week, attached to an IV that pumped fluid through her body. Her medication chart filled an entire A4 page, with a dose of 20 tablets each day. At times it took Angela two hours to get her to take all of the medication. She hid the tablets in marshmallows or cheese for a while, until Blaze stopped eating those too.

For a while, Angela's entire wages were going to pay for Blaze's care. In a bid to help raise a few dollars, Angela even put Blaze's favourite star toy up for sale on TradeMe. It sold for $150, and others donated money or sent toys. Someone even made a blanket especially for Blaze.

Blaze's condition is now improving, with biopsies showing that her liver is slowly healing — something the vets never thought would be possible. However, Blaze still takes medicine twice a day and probably will have to for the rest of her life. She has also developed a skin condition that requires more medication and a special diet. However, her zest for life and toys continues, and Angela will keep doing whatever it takes to be sure she is happy.

For a while, Angela's entire wages were going to pay for Blaze's care.

Stevie

Stevie was just six months old when her family's house was red-zoned. They had to move into an apartment where pets weren't allowed, and for a few days they kept Stevie in the car, wondering where they could take her.

Then they saw a notice on the Dogwatch website that HUHA was making a third mercy mission to rescue 26 Christchurch dogs and re-home them in Wellington.

Vari, a HUHA trustee, and her daughter, TJ, were part of the HUHA volunteer delegation on that third trip. Vari was inside Dogwatch doing paperwork and TJ was out in the yard holding dogs when a woman and her teenage daughter dropped off Stevie. The daughter was extremely upset to have to let the gorgeous Labrador-cross puppy go. TJ couldn't believe

what a cute puppy she was and knew it would be easy to find her a new home in Wellington.

Once on the truck, most of the dogs were scared and anxious, but Stevie seemed excited to be there. She had to be given extra doses of Rescue Remedy because she had so much energy.

TJ was right that such a gorgeous fawn ball of fluff would be snapped up quickly. On arriving in Wellington, Stevie was adopted straight away. However, a few days later, the woman rang HUHA in tears. She said that Stevie was too rough and described her

as a 'coiled spring', waiting to explode.

Vari and TJ went to pick up Stevie that night. They managed to contain her energy just long enough to get her into the back of the car. They walked around to the front, and there was Stevie in the driver's seat, wriggling with excitement at seeing them again so soon!

Vari and her family already had a one-year-old puppy, so adding another bundle of energy to their lives was hard work. After a couple of weeks, they found a lovely family in Auckland who wanted to adopt Stevie. Vari knew they would give her a great home, but after getting to know Stevie, Vari was having second thoughts about sending this very high-energy pup so far away, in case she became too much to handle and they needed to reclaim her again.

Meanwhile, Vari's husband Marc had secretly fallen for Stevie, as she reminded him of their 16-year-old dog Chilli, who had recently died. So when Vari mentioned that she had found another home for Stevie, Marc suggested that they keep her instead. Vari didn't have to be asked twice. Stevie has now settled in nicely and loves playing with the other animals on the 1.4 hectare lifestyle block.

Stevie was one of more than 70 dogs that HUHA successfully re-homed in Wellington and further afield in the North Island, showing the huge support and concern throughout New Zealand for Christchurch families and their dogs.

Stevie was one of more than 70 dogs that HUHA successfully re-homed.

Faye

Faye is an extremely timid, three-year-old miniature schnauzer-Shetland sheepdog cross. On 22 February 2011, Faye was home alone when the earthquake hit. She was terrified, but luckily her owner Jeremy's work was nearby and he quickly biked home. Faye immediately clung to him like superglue.

Over two hours later, Jeremy's partner, Rachel, was still not home. Jeremy wanted to go and look for her on his bike, but he didn't want to leave Faye home alone with so many aftershocks occurring. He took Faye to his parents' house, where his mother Elaine was huddled with a group of friends.

Faye was uneasy with people she didn't know, but as long as she stayed close to Elaine, she was settled. Unfortunately, just when Elaine had to go to the toilet and Faye was left behind with strangers, an aftershock hit. One of the women panicked and opened the back door. Faye bolted outside and ran down the street as fast as her little legs would move. Elaine ran after her for several blocks, screaming her name in desperation, but Faye just kept running. By the time she stopped, she must have had no idea where she was or how to get home.

When Rachel and Jeremy found out that Faye had escaped, they too tried to follow her escape route, but by then the trail was cold. They got in contact with the rest of their family

in Christchurch and organised a search party. They scoured her favourite parks like police investigating a crime scene, searching in line formation so they wouldn't miss any clues. They fanned out across the neighbourhood, knocking on doors and peering into back yards and under bushes.

By that night, they felt defeated but didn't give up hope. They put ads on TradeMe and Pets On The Net, and the next day they posted 200 flyers in areas where they thought Faye might go.

Over the next three days, they received numerous phone calls from people who had spotted Faye all over the western side of the city, from Fendalton to Bishopdale to Riccarton. The callers all said that Faye had been running fast and she couldn't be caught.

Although Rachel's work at the SPCA was the busiest it had ever been, with an influx of animals needing help, all she could think about was Faye. Every night she and Jeremy went out looking for her until it was dark.

On 25 February, Rachel was getting ready for work, when she heard a weird whining noise outside. She went to the front door and realised it was coming from outside the front gate. She rushed out to find a filthy, absolutely exhausted but ecstatic Faye. After three days of wandering, she had finally found her way home.

Rachel took Faye into the SPCA for a check-up, and when they got back home the rest of the family came over to see her. Faye greeted every person as if she had missed them terribly. She chattered away with whimpers and whines, trying to tell of her adventures around the city. Once everyone had gone, she collapsed and slept like she had never slept before, for 14 hours straight.

Blue

By Joe Bennett

I got Blue from the pound as a puppy. He was scared of big dogs, though he pretended otherwise, and of being excluded from car trips. But unlike any dog I'd had before, he wasn't scared of thunder or of fireworks or even, when they first struck, of earthquakes.

On the morning of 4 September 2010 he came into the bedroom after the first quake to see if things were all right. They were, so he went back to his armchair in the living room. During the numerous aftershocks he merely looked up at me. I have found that the best way to reassure a dog is to carry on as normal.

But on 22 February 2011 we were close to the epicentre. The quake hit like a rifle shot. Blue fled the house and stood shaking in the garden. A few minutes later an aftershock saw him leap the fence and pick a fight with the neighbour's dog. Then he ran away. He had never done any of these things before. Five minutes later I got a call from a friend who lives on the other side of Lyttelton. Blue had run there.

Twenty months have passed since then. Blue's spent a lot of them in the car. I leave it permanently open in the garage. It's become his refuge, his den. Like a den, it's low-roofed, enclosing, dark. And unlike a house it has shock absorbers.

He is in there now, at 11 on a Saturday morning, curled in the

It's become his refuge, his den. Like a den, it's low-roofed, enclosing, dark. And unlike a house it has shock absorbers.

driver's seat, his head flopped over the handbrake. When I make lunch shortly, he'll join me in the house. After lunch I'll take him out on the hills, then feed him. But once he's sure the good things are over, he'll spend the afternoon in the car.

Thunder now terrifies him, fireworks too, and he's alarmed even by the distant thud of containers being loaded on the wharf. And he doesn't like to be alone. I doubt he'll ever lose those traits now. The aftershocks went on for too long. But he's my dog, and I love him and he still relishes the world when it isn't shaking. We'll be fine.

Cairo

Cairo is a seven-year-old 'very mixed breed' that bounded into Janelle's life as a bold and cheeky black puppy. At the time, Janelle had just lost her dog Kahlie, who died suddenly and unexpectedly just a week after becoming certified as a USAR dog.

Still reeling from the loss, Janelle was far from looking for a new puppy, but when pound manager and USAR national trainer, Brenda, asked her to take the energetic pup for a weekend, she agreed.

On the Monday, Janelle returned the pup to the pound, but she couldn't get him out of her mind. After a few days, she rang back and took the pup home again — just for the time being. She gave him the interim name Appro (as in 'on appro'). Eventually, this morphed into Cairo, which stuck, and Cairo the dog stuck around too. Cairo became an operational USAR dog two years later.

On 22 February 2011, Janelle was in Wellington at an emergency-management conference. When rumours of another Christchurch quake were confirmed, she went straight to the airport. Commercial flights were all grounded, but she managed to hitch a ride south on a chartered plane bringing other emergency officials and medical supplies.

Cairo and Janelle's other dog

Chilli were staying at a kennel near Kaiapoi, and the owners knew as soon as the quake hit that Cairo would be needed. When Janelle drove up later that afternoon, they immediately appeared.

'We've been expecting you,' they said. 'Cairo has had dinner and is all ready to go. Just leave Chilli with us.' Within two minutes Janelle and Cairo were packed up and ready to go.

They got home in the late afternoon to find their house so surrounded by liquefaction that the garage door wouldn't open. The keys were in the lock inside the front door, so Janelle had to get a crowbar and smash a front window to get in. They were soon on their way into the city to get to work.

One of the first buildings they searched was a church, the roof of which was being held up by a crane. By that stage it was dark, and the site was a tangle of glass, wire and steel. Just as they were about to enter, the generator cut out and plunged them into complete blackness. It was a horror situation, but the search had

to continue. They got other rescue workers to turn their torches on the site and continued the search as best they could.

Later that night, they were searching a shop that had collapsed under the weight of the next-door bakery. Using her torch, Janelle saw a giant red smear on the wall and cringed. She had a policeman investigate more closely.

He came back to her smiling. 'It's raspberry jam,' he said with a sigh of relief.

Cairo continued his search and came across a soft, cream-coloured pile on the ground. Janelle again recoiled and had the policeman inspect. After a closer look, he said, 'We have pikelets to go with our jam.'

Cairo's greatest skill during this work was breaking and entering. If anything was blocking a search site and needed to be pushed aside, Cairo was the dog for the job. His strength, endurance, agility and experience made him a valuable member of the USAR team.

Milo

Milo was just 10 weeks old when he was found abandoned in a locked shed with his brother and sister after the 22 February 2011 earthquake. The house to which the shed belonged had been destroyed in the earthquake and Milo's owners had disappeared.

No one knows how long the Labrador–huntaway cross puppies had been left on their own, but they were in a very sorry state by the time they were found.

Milo and his brother and sister were taken to Dogwatch, but because the pups were so anxious during the aftershocks, they were top candidates when Dogwatch was deciding which dogs to send with HUHA to be re-homed in Wellington.

Meanwhile, Nikki and her family heard about the HUHA mission to rescue 24 dogs from Christchurch, and decided they wanted to help. Like many families around Wellington, all of whom had other pets, commitments and responsibilities, they were ready to open their hearts and homes to help the dogs of Christchurch.

On 25 June 2011, Nikki and her family waited along with HUHA volunteers and other adopting families for the HUHA truck to arrive at the Moa Point pound. It was a freezing cold winter's day, with horizontal rain and a howling wind, but there was still an atmosphere of excitement, as everyone waited for the dogs to arrive.

The families hadn't been 'assigned' a particular dog beforehand, but they had seen photos of some of the dogs. Nikki and her family had thought a German shepherd cross looked nice, but it turned out she wasn't good with farm animals. They needed a dog that wouldn't have issues with the many other animals on their lifestyle block such as sheep, free-range chickens and cats.

When the HUHA truck arrived, a volunteer told them to take some of the dogs for a walk and see which ones caught their eye. Nikki's family walked a golden retriever, but she was very strong and Nikki worried about what she would be like with their other two male dogs.

Then Nikki saw Milo's sweet face looking up at her from the back of his crate, where he was cowering. He was very frightened and didn't want to walk on a lead, but she knew instantly that this was the dog for them. They wrapped him in a blanket to take him home to Otaki.

On the journey home, they bought a takeaway hot chocolate to warm up. As soon as Milo got a whiff, he perked right up. He has always had an amazing appetite and even now it's a race between him and the family's golden retriever Bobby as to who can finish meals first.

Milo latched onto Nikki immediately. He was very nervous around both men and other dogs, and it took him a little while to get used to the family's other dogs, Bobby and Sam, and the cats, Disco and Disney. However, Bobby and Sam were very gentle with him and it didn't take long for Milo to enjoy having other dogs to play with again.

Milo is still wary of strangers and other dogs, but with his family he is completely content and very playful. He loves walking on the beach, and Nikki has never had to walk him on a lead as he is too scared to go very far away from her. He thinks he belongs on everyone's lap, even though he is now a bit big for that. He also can't sleep alone, and although he has his own bed, Milo always jumps onto Sam's bed to snuggle up with the older dog for the night.

Jet

Jet, a six-year-old Labrador, was at home with a house-sitter when the 4 September 2010 earthquake hit. The house-sitter, who was pregnant, fell down the stairs in her haste to escape, and in a panic locked Jet inside the house.

Jet's owners Caroline and Bruce were away that weekend, and as soon as they found out what had happened, they rang their daughter Kylie and asked her to go and pick up Jet. Jet was alone inside for two and a half hours as Kylie drove what would normally have been a five-minute trip. The Dallington bridge was impassable and the roads were full of water and potholes.

When Kylie arrived, she found Jet peering out through the door with a teddy bear in her mouth. The house was a shambles. Jet's bed was covered in glass and ornaments from a shelf unit that had come crashing down.

Kylie brought Jet back to her house, where she would stay until Caroline and Bruce returned. Jet was used to staying at Kylie's, since she often went there for sleepovers. Her favourite part of those visits was always the black cat, Tiger. Jet and Tiger were inseparable, following each other around by day and curling up to sleep together at night.

So Jet was horrified to get to Kylie's and find that Tiger was nowhere

to be found. Kylie and Jet went out searching for him in all of his favourite haunts. Jet sniffed through the bushes, trying to find her lost friend's scent. No luck, so they took the car to search more widely, but there was still no sign of Tiger.

Kylie and Jet returned home downhearted, but when Kylie opened the car door, Jet's eyes lit up. She bounded out of the car and ran to the gate where a demure Tiger stood quietly, apparently unmoved as Jet licked his face joyously.

After the September quake, Jet developed severe separation anxiety. She followed Kylie everywhere, wanting to be with her even when she was in the toilet or shower. If she was left alone, she would whimper and cry until someone came to rescue her. She knew when an aftershock was about to hit and would lick Kylie's hand in warning. An avid swimmer, she now wanted to avoid water and stayed well clear of her usual swimming spots in the river and at the beach.

When the 22 February 2011 quake hit Jet was back at home, but this time she was outside in the yard on her own. Liquefaction completely covered the entire yard so Jet could hardly find a place to stand. She stood by the gate, teddy in mouth, for three hours until Caroline could finally make her way home.

As time passes and memories of the big quakes fade, Jet's separation anxiety has eased and she doesn't mind staying at home alone now. The fate of her home is still unknown, as one side has slumped into an old watercourse, but Jet remains blissfully unaware, enjoying her swims and sleepovers with Tiger.

Kizzy

On 22 February 2011, Kizzy had a litter of five three-week-old puppies. The seven-year-old Boston terrier had just been feeding the pups and was in another room having a meal of her own when the earthquake struck. The shaking brought a giant trophy on the shelf above the whelping box tumbling over, missing the pups by just inches.

With the floor still rolling and objects flying, Kizzy frantically ran to find her puppies. The door to the pups' room was closed, and she threw herself at it, desperate to reach them.

It was several minutes before owner Val was able to stand up and wade through the debris to open the door. Kizzy ran to the whelping box and, finding all of the pups undamaged (and still fast asleep), she hunkered down, not moving during the many strong aftershocks that followed.

For three long weeks after the February quake, Val and her husband David had no water. Every day they gathered as many containers as they could find and made the long journey over potholed streets to Pioneer Stadium to get water, which they desperately needed not only for themselves but also for Kizzy and her pups.

To make things even more complicated, about five days after the big quake Kizzy's milk suddenly dried up. The vet said it was common for lactating dogs to react this way under stress. Val put out an emergency call for anyone who might have dog milk

that they could spare, but the only response was from Nelson, too far for them to travel. Val tried feeding the pups Royal Canin milk powder from a bottle, but the pups were too used to feeding from Kizzy to willingly accept a substitute.

Boston terriers are a very difficult dog to breed, and Val knew she had to do everything she could to keep the pups alive. The only option was for Val and David to feed the pups using a syringe. The syringe would only hold a tiny amount of powdered milk, however, so they had to feed the pups every two hours, day and night.

Kizzy got her milk back about six days later, but by that time Val was exhausted from the gruelling feeding routine — on top of aftershocks and difficulties getting water — and she just needed to get away. She searched for a bach on TradeMe and found a family that was offering free accommodation at their house in Oamaru for shaken Christchurch residents.

Val emailed Bob and Linda Wilson on a whim — she was fairly certain accommodating a dog, let alone a litter of five puppies, would be too much to ask — but she quickly received an email reply saying they could all come down and stay as long as they wanted. Val burst into tears. She couldn't believe that complete strangers could be so trusting and generous.

But Val and David had an even better surprise in store. They arrived at the address they had been given to find a magnificent Oamaru stone house set on a hectare of impeccably manicured gardens. It was too good to be true. They spent seven days enjoying the beautiful surroundings, the lack of aftershocks and, best of all, as much water as they needed.

The unknown dog

Following the 22 February 2011 quake, Liz and her colleagues were walking down Armagh Street towards Hagley Park, being evacuated from the CBD. As they walked, they met many hurt, crying and traumatised people, but one woman in particular got Liz's attention. She was walking a dog on a lead and carrying something in her other hand.

Liz started talking to the woman, as she was going the same direction as them. The dog was limping slightly and was covered in dust, so Liz asked her if the dog was OK.

'I don't know,' she replied with a dazed expression. Puzzled, Liz waited for some further explanation.

'It's not my dog. I found him in a car that was crushed by one of the buildings.'

It was then Liz realised the woman was carrying a licence plate in her other hand.

'The dog's owner didn't make it, so I took the number plate off the car in the hope that when I get home, I can try to use the registration plate number to find the dog's family.'

And with those words, she headed off across Hagley Park with the dog, head down, limping behind her.

Buster

On 22 February 2011, Buster, a three-year-old Staffie-pit bull cross, was at home lying on the front step, as he often did. He was a good dog and never tried to run away, so there was no need for fences or chains. When the shaking started, though, everything changed.

Buster bolted. He ran and ran and ran, and only stopped when his paws were so raw and sore that he couldn't run any further.

Buster was found later that evening hiding beside a bakery, many kilometres from home. A kind woman gave him a pie and a drink and rang the SPCA.

Meanwhile, Buster's owner Hayden had walked home from work because his car was stuck in liquefaction. When he got home and found Buster was missing, a horrible feeling grew in the pit of his stomach. Buster had never wandered nor spent a single day away from him.

Hayden, his partner Charlotte and some of their family set out by bike to search the neighbourhood. When they told someone they were looking for a Staffie–pit bull cross, he replied, 'A Staffie? You won't find him again in this neighbourhood.'

The next day they went to the SPCA and told them they were looking for a Staffie, but the SPCA told them they didn't have any dogs of that breed. Little did Hayden and Charlotte know that Buster was

indeed out the back, just metres away.

For the next five days, Charlotte and Hayden visited the pound several times each day. Going to the SPCA meant a difficult journey to the other side of the broken city, so it wasn't until day five that they could make that trip again.

This time they told the SPCA they were looking for a Staffie–pit bull cross. Bingo! The SPCA staff told them they had a dog who was injured and that they had isolated him out the back. They suspected he had ringworm, because of a circular bald patch on the top of his head. When they said this, Hayden knew it had to be Buster, as he had an infected scratch from a run-in with a big tabby several weeks prior that had caused a bald patch on his head.

Hayden walked out the back but the only dog he could see was too skinny and meek to be Buster. He walked up to the dog, who looked up at him with no sense of recognition.

'No, it's not him,' Hayden thought. And then he spotted the bald patch on the top of his head.

'Buster?' he said. A light went on in Buster's eyes as if to say 'It's you!' He jumped up, barked and ran in circles.

Buster was very happy to go home, but his adventures had taken a toll. The pads on his paws were completely torn off, leaving raw, bloody wounds. The vet gave him little yellow socks to wear, but Buster soon took them off, finding them too slippery to walk in.

His paws eventually healed, but his hips seem to have been permanently damaged. He can't walk for more than 30 minutes now. Buster is also extremely wary of people, and he has lost his once confident, trusting nature. He is terrified of aftershocks and will stop crying only when Charlotte and Hayden put him in the car and drive until he falls asleep, curled up on Charlotte's lap in the passenger seat.

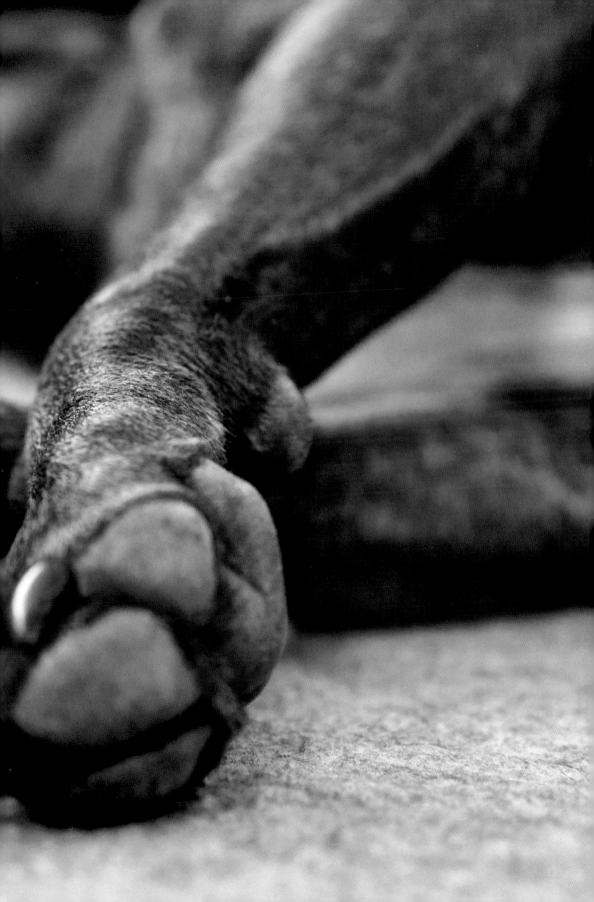

Otis

Otis is an eight-year-old German shepherd with a full-time job as a police dog. Tim has been training Otis since he was a young pup, first as a front-line police dog and later for search and rescue and victim recovery. To do his job well, Otis must be hard-working, focused, highly driven and confident.

For five years, Otis worked on the front line with Tim, hunting burglars and helping to solve crimes. However, a few years ago when Tim took up a role as the police puppy development officer for Canterbury, Otis was relegated to the occasional callout for search-and-rescue or victim-recovery jobs. He began to get bored and frustrated.

Then the 4 September 2010 earthquake struck. Tim and Otis were quickly sent back to the front line. Otis was happy to be back at work with Tim rather than stuck at home alone.

When the 22 February 2011 quake hit, Tim had just returned from lunch to his van across from the main police station. When the van began to shake, he thought it was just Otis and the other dogs moving around in the back. He quickly realised his mistake.

For the 24 hours following the quake, Otis was the only qualified victim-recovery dog in Canterbury. Unlike USAR dogs, victim-recovery dogs are trained to locate dead bodies. Finding the exact location of the deceased is important so that their remains can be carefully

recovered from large piles of rubble.

Otis knows it is time to start searching when Tim puts his special search collar on him. The dogs work in pairs, with one dog searching at a time. If the first dog indicates, the second dog is brought in to confirm the find. Otis's signal for finding someone is to sit or lie down and bark. Unlike many police dogs, Otis works without a lead so that he can reach into nooks and crannies.

Otis made several memorable and important finds after the February quake. Alongside a LandSAR team, Otis and Tim helped find three victims in a church. They also located two people crushed under a fallen store awning and one killed by a large boulder that crashed down through their house from the hills above.

During the first week, Otis and Tim worked 130 hours and did hundreds of searches. They were the only local victim-recovery team, so while the rest of the handlers would take their dogs to the police kennels and go to a hotel each night, Otis and Tim would return home. Each morning they had to switch gears as they went back through the cordon, like a portal into a parallel world.

Otis is now living in Auckland with his new handler, Colin, and he is again working as a victim-recovery dog. He also goes with Colin on school visits, showing off his skills for fighting dangerous criminals by attacking a padded sleeve. When he retires in the next couple of years, he will give up his day job for life as a normal family pet.

Lola

Nothing is known about exactly what happened to Lola, a three-year-old Labrador–Staffie cross, when the 22 February 2011 quake hit. Perhaps her home was destroyed and her family fled, like so many Cantabrians. Or perhaps she ran away and her family couldn't find her.

Whatever tragedy befell her, by March 2011 she was another earth-quake orphan on death row at the Christchurch pound.

Dogwatch saw what a lovely-natured dog Lola was and saved her from being put down. However, like all animal shelters in Christchurch, Dogwatch was bursting at the seams. They were desperate to find homes for some of their dogs, to make way for the many others that needed to be saved.

Lola had been at Dogwatch for only about a week when Cherie, a volunteer at HUHA, arrived in Christchurch. Cherie was helping to organise HUHA's first rescue mission to take stray and abandoned cats, as well as roosters and turtles, up to Wellington to be re-homed. She fell in love with Lola's sweet smile and offered to take her and another dog back with them to Wellington, as they had two homes ready to adopt them.

A few days later, Cherie piled Lola and Jessie into the back of the van and started the journey north to Picton. She had been on the road only a few minutes when she got a phone

call from a family in Wellington that was looking to adopt a dog. As she spoke with them, she realised that she had just left the perfect dog for them back at Dogwatch. She did a U-turn and returned to pick up this dog, named Archie. She piled him in the back with Lola and Jessie and set out for Picton again. Despite being told to keep the dogs apart because they didn't get along, Lola and Jessie sat together in the front seat next to Cherie while Archie relaxed in the back.

When Lola got to Wellington she was taken directly to her new home, but she was so energetic that she soon became too challenging for the family, who had young children. She would chew the children's toys and shoes while they were out, and even long runs would not calm her down. After a couple of weeks Lola was sent back to Cherie, who kept her for a week until HUHA could find her a new home.

Lola needed to be with someone who could spend a lot of time with her and could handle her high energy levels. Carolyn, HUHA's founder, thought of a family friend, Linda, who had lost her own dog recently. When Carolyn rang her, Linda said it was still too soon, but Carolyn convinced her that she should try Lola 'just for the weekend, and if it's not right you can bring her back'.

On Sunday night, Linda sent Carolyn a text message: 'I guess she's staying. I've just bought a big bag of dog food.'

Linda and Lola are now inseparable, and Lola loves running on the beach and playing with other dogs, especially her best mate, Bella the miniature poodle. Lola was one of the lucky earthquake orphans to find a loving home that will care for her for the rest of her days.

Linda and Lola are now inseparable.

Caiou, Chloe & Little

Caiou the greyhound, Chloe the chihuahua, and Little the Labrador cross were home alone when the 22 February 2011 quake hit. The whole house was like a washing machine. The coffee machine flew into the lounge and the dishwasher ended up in the dining room.

Little was in his bed, where he always lay during the day, when a huge cabinet toppled over and was about to fall on top of him. To avoid a certain and excruciating death, he dove headfirst through a glass door.

Caiou and Chloe were thrilled that Little had created an escape route. After the tremors subsided, they followed Little out into the garden and huddled together in a safe corner. Little had a large chunk of glass jutting from his forehead.

Meanwhile, their owner Elena, an animal physiotherapist, was working at a vet clinic in town. When the quake struck, all of the animals at the clinic shrieked and howled. Not realising how severe the quake had been, Elena agreed to stay and help calm the patients until their owners could get there.

It was not until Elena got in her car and started driving home a few hours later that she realised just how much damage the quake had caused. She then had a text message from her husband, Andy, telling her the Ferrymead bridge was closed and he couldn't get home. At that moment,

she began to panic about how Caiou, Chloe and Little had fared.

Knowing she had to find an alternative route to Sumner, Elena set off cross-country. She drove up to Summit Road and then down a farm track onto Clifton Hill above Sumner. Boulders were whizzing past but she barely noticed.

When she finally got home, the house was a shambles and the dogs were nowhere to be seen. She saw the broken door and feared the worst. She ran to a neighbour's house to see if she had seen the dogs, and there in the garden was Andy with the three dogs. A big tan bandage was wrapped around Little's ears and under his chin.

Several hours earlier, Andy had managed to get home after all, by parking at the Ferrymead bridge and running the remaining 5 kilometres home. He had found all three dogs huddled together, with the piece of glass still stuck in Little's forehead, blood dripping down his head and neck. Luckily, as a trained vet, Andy knew how to remove the glass and bandage the wound.

After his narrow escape Little's coat turned a bit grey, but he has been relatively calm during the aftershocks and, now that he has a dog door, he doesn't mind being left inside. Caiou is the most sensitive of the three dogs, and he comes running to Elena whenever there is a shake or loud noise. Chloe has been the toughest — although it helps that she is usually being held or carried in Elena's handbag.

Shi

Eight-year-old English Staffie Shi has two best friends: Mary Jane, a small grey moggie, and Norma Jean, a spotted Bengal cat. Mary Jane and Norma Jean were born just two months before the 22 February 2011 earthquake. Shi instantly took a liking to the two kittens, looking after them as if they were her own puppies.

When the February earthquake hit, Norma Jean — like many other cats around the city — disappeared. Shi was distraught. She spent hours searching the house and garden, pacing back and forth. When Norma Jean finally reappeared three days later, Shi seemed determined to do something to ease the kittens' anxiety.

A few days later, Shi began producing milk. She encouraged the kittens to nurse, and soon it became a regular habit. Shi would search for the kittens to get them to feed several times each day. They would all end up in a furry pile on her bed, Shi snoring, the kittens nursing and all three completely content.

It was an amusing and unusual distraction from an otherwise dire situation at Anna's house in Aranui. They had no power or water for weeks, eventually getting power back to only half of the house. Sewage leaked into their backyard, so that even when water came back on, it was unpleasant to use the toilet or washing machine. Many of their neighbours moved out, one abandoning a pet goat that the

remaining neighbours adopted as a symbol of their determination to keep their cul-de-sac community alive despite the devastation.

Shi continued to take her maternal responsibilities seriously, nursing Mary Jane and Norma Jean for four months, until Anna and Shi finally moved out of the broken Aranui house. The kittens stayed behind with Anna's daughter for six more weeks, which Anna thought would break the nursing routine. But as soon as the animals were reunited, Shi launched wholeheartedly back into her maternal duties.

It wasn't until a year later, when Shi came into heat, that she finally stopped nursing 'her babies'. Norma Jean stayed with Shi in her bed the whole time she was in labour, watching as she gave birth to four beautiful puppies. Shi now had a new brood to care for, but she didn't forget her kittens, still sleeping with them and tracking their movements to be sure they didn't disappear again.

Max

Max, a bull mastiff–pit bull cross was just a pup when the 22 February 2011 quake hit. His family's home in Hornby was damaged badly, and, although they stayed there as long as they could, they were eventually forced to move out.

They couldn't find rental accommodation that would take an inside dog that was growing bigger by the day, so they gave him to whanau to look after. Sadly, none of them was allowed to have dogs either, and so he was passed from house to house as each successive landlord found out about him. Eventually, there were no more homes left in which Max could hide.

At this stage, Max's family knew they had exhausted all of their options. They rang Trisha at K9 Rescue to ask about re-homing Max.

They desperately didn't want to give him away, but they had tried everything they could think of to keep him. When they dropped Max off, the young girl in the family hugged Max and started crying. Her mum had to pry her arms from around his neck.

Max had come from such a loving family that Trisha was determined to find him a great new home. Her friend Kristin had been looking for a dog for some time, and Trisha thought it could be just the right spot for Max. Kristin and her kids, Saskia-

lee and Taison, would give Max all the love and care that his previous family had.

When Trisha rang Kristin to tell her she had found the perfect dog for her, Kristin was a little apprehensive. Although she had fostered some dogs for Trisha in the past, she had never had a dog of her own. She agreed to foster Max first, and if they got along she would then adopt him.

The week before Max came to live with Kristin, her house was broken into and burgled. Being on her own with two young children, Kristin was a nervous wreck. She spent nights on the couch in the lounge, waking up frequently with every little noise. When Max arrived, she suddenly felt much safer. Kristin was able to sleep through the night for the first time since their house was robbed. She felt as though Max had saved them just as much as they had saved him.

Kristin soon knew that Max was indeed the perfect dog for them, and told Trisha they would be Max's forever home. Although he is big and strong, he can also be very gentle, especially with Saskia-lee and Taison.

The sea was a strange new phenomenon for Max, and at first he would just stand on the beach and watch the children splash in the waves. Walks on the beach are now his favourite part of the day, and he bravely ventures into the sea for a splash and a play.

She felt as though Max had saved them just as much as they had saved him.

Sasha

Sara found Sasha, a huntaway-border collie cross, at the Auckland SPCA in 2005, when Sasha and her brothers and sisters were just 10 weeks old. Sara walked up to their kennel, and Sasha was the first to curiously approach her. However, one of her brothers promptly came up and pushed her out of the way and then one of her sisters came to have a look.

Sara was worried that Sasha's extreme cuteness might blind her to any potential flaws she might have as a USAR dog, so she tested her brother and sister first by giving them toys to see how driven they were to play with them. They were very sweet little pups but they soon lost interest in the toys, which indicated that they had little drive. Sara then put Sasha into the playpen, and Sasha became completely absorbed in playing with the toys even when Sara banged pots and pans around her. Sara saw that Sasha had the drive it would take to become a good USAR dog.

Sasha was certified as a USAR dog when she was just two years old. She trained around Auckland with other USAR and LandSAR dogs, and had two deployments before the 22 February 2011 earthquake: to a house collapse in South Auckland in 2009 and to the September 2010 Canterbury earthquake.

On 22 February 2011, Sara was at work when she heard news of the big quake, and she immediately knew that they would be called to duty.

She and Sasha went to Task Force 3's headquarters in Auckland, one of the three USAR task force bases set up in New Zealand to mobilise when an emergency strikes. From there, they received a police escort to the Whenuapai air force base. Around 100 task force members flew down to Christchurch, arriving in the evening and then working in the CBD through the night.

Over the next three days, Sasha worked incredibly hard. She wasn't drinking or eating enough and wasn't getting enough sleep, as they were doing night shifts and trying to sleep during the day in the busy tent camp in Latimer Square.

On the third day, after a major search, Sasha snacked on some rotten food in one of the collapsed buildings. As a precaution, Sara took her to an emergency vet and she was put on fluids for 12 hours to rehydrate. The team watched her closely to be sure she was just exhausted and hadn't eaten anything toxic.

The next day Sasha was much better and began to eat and drink on her own. At this point, Sara decided that Sasha needed time to recover. After their seven days of hard work, it was time to return to Auckland.

Sasha is now retired from USAR and enjoying life as a normal pet dog. Every now and then she enjoys a 'fun find' but mostly she just takes pleasure in swimming, playing frisbee and relaxing in the sun.

Sophie & Rev

22 February 2011 was just like any other normal Tuesday for dog walker and trainer Dennis and his dogs, Sophie, a huntaway, and Rev, a huntaway-heading dog cross. In the morning, Dennis took Sophie and eight other dogs on their regular morning walk, and at lunchtime they returned to their Brighton home to pick up Rev for their afternoon walk.

Dennis let Sophie into the house and scattered some nibbles for her. He collected Rev and had just left the house when the earthquake struck. As furniture and objects crashed around Sophie, she hid under a small table, her world literally falling down around her. Rev bolted down the drive and tried to get into the van with the other dogs. The dogs in the van were completely unperturbed, perhaps since they were used to bouncing around in it.

Dennis rescued a shivering Sophie from under the table, grabbed Rev and plonked them both into the van with the other dogs. Landlines were down and cell phone networks were overloaded, so Dennis couldn't reach any of the other dogs' families. He decided the safest place to go would be Waimairi Beach, which was completely deserted when they arrived. He walked the dogs on the beach for several hours, watching the aftershocks roll through the sand and sea.

Later, Dennis transferred all of the dogs from the van to his four-wheel-drive, which he figured he would

need in order to make it through the deep water and liquefaction around the city. Dennis made his way slowly from house to house, delivering the dogs to their homes. Where the families were at home, there was a happy reunion, but if no one was home, the dogs stayed with Dennis.

By the time the trip was finished, Dennis still had two of the eight dogs with him, plus the shaken Sophie and Rev. The four dogs slept with Dennis that night, one at each corner of the bed. It was a long night with no power, no water and no news.

One of the dog-walking dogs stayed for a week until his family was able to take him home, and the other ended up staying for four months while one member of her family recovered from severe injuries. A third dog, Manu, also joined the clan for eight months when her family's house was declared uninhabitable and she had nowhere else to go.

Sophie still gets anxious during aftershocks, but Rev has been the most affected by the continuing shakes. When the 23 December 2011 earthquake struck, Dennis's wife, Yolanda, was out walking with Rev and he was so frightened that she had to lift him into the car. Once home, he wouldn't get out again.

Vehicles became the dogs' favourite refuge for many weeks after the quakes. During these periods, Rev became completely inactive and would barely drink or eat. Even treats wouldn't tempt him. Homeopathy helped to ease Rev's anxiety, but two years later he is still always on edge.

Emiko

Two days after the 22 February 2011 earthquake, Francesca returned home from a run to find a gorgeous jet-black puppy wandering around her front yard. For half an hour she walked up and down the street looking for the pup's owner, to no avail. She brought the puppy inside and gave her some food and water.

Not knowing what else to do, Fran decided to let the pup stay the night, thinking that in the morning she would call the pound. The pup spent the night curled up on her flatmate Martin's bed, crying and whining.

When Animal Control officers picked up the pup from her house the next day, Francesca found it heart-breaking to say goodbye, but she knew she couldn't have a dog. First of all, she was not a dog person at all. She was scared of dogs and would cross the road if she met one that looked unsavoury. Also, she had a demanding job where she worked long hours, and was planning to go on her OE in Canada soon.

But over the next week, Francesca found herself ringing the pound every day to see if anyone had claimed the pup. On the seventh day, when the owner still hadn't showed up, she drove to the pound and, without a second thought, brought the young pup home. She named the three-month-old Staffie–Labrador cross Emiko, which means 'beautiful girl' in Japanese.

Since Francesca had never had a

dog before, she didn't know what to feed it, what supplies she needed, where it would sleep or how to train it. Luckily, Emiko was a clever dog and she already had the basics down pat. She went outside to poo and wee, and climbed on the furniture only when she was told she could. To Francesca's surprise, Emiko even waited until she was told she could eat when her bowl of food was placed in front of her. She refused to drink water from a bowl and would only slurp from a running tap.

Everyone now tells Francesca that Emiko came to the right home. She and Emiko go running together every day, and on Fridays flatmate Martin takes Emiko to a farm, where she plays with the other animals and runs wildly through the paddocks. She is learning lots of tricks, like giving high-fives and playing dead when someone points at her and yells 'bang bang'. Her passion and obsession is her ball and, although she won't go near the sea or rivers, she loves being sprayed with the hose in the back garden.

Stanley & Jack

Stanley, an eight-year-old Airedale–bearded collie cross, and Jack, a nine-year-old fox terrier–bearded collie cross, are an inseparable team. On 22 February 2011, they were at home in Somerfield with Sharon when the quake struck.

Sharon managed to get both of them into the car, but before she could drive away, the car became stuck in deep liquefaction. She left Stanley and Jack in the car and got a neighbour to take her to the school to pick up her son, Angus.

When Sharon and Angus returned, it was clear their home was unsafe to occupy. They packed up their most critical belongings and went to stay with Sharon's parents for a few days. They had no idea how long they would be out of their home. Rental accommodation was scarce, and finding a place that would allow two dogs was virtually impossible.

During the next year, Stanley, Jack, Angus and Sharon moved seven times. A kind friend took them in for three months, until Sharon found a kennel in Nelson that agreed to take Stanley and Jack for a couple of months. Sharon and Angus moved to her brother's house in Nelson to be close to them.

Not wanting to take advantage of the generosity of the kennel owners, their next move was to a donkey farm in Oxford. Stanley and Jack

loved the farm, as they had plenty of space to run, they liked playing with the donkeys and there were few aftershocks out there.

Again, however, it was only a temporary situation, and Stanley and Jack's next port of call was the Kosy K9s kennel in Rangiora. Sharon and Angus moved into the nearby campground. Sharon remembers this as a desperate time.

When summer came, the kennel was fully booked, so it was time for Stanley and Jack to pack their bags again. This time Sharon put an advertisement in the paper and a generous person in Spencerville agreed to look after them for two and a half months.

By this stage, Sharon and Angus were completely exhausted from the many moves. Angus had changed schools four times. They decided they needed to go home no matter what. They found a huge canvas tent and set it up in the small back garden. They dragged extension cords from the house and made their 'glamping' site as comfortable as possible.

Just as another winter was approaching and Sharon was wondering what they would do next, she had a phone call from the contractors to say that their house would be fixed and it would take six to eight weeks for the repairs to be completed. Sharon and Angus moved everything out of the house and into the garage in preparation. They could move in with Sharon's parents for a couple of months until the repairs were done, but again the problem was what to do with Stanley and Jack. Sharon decided to leave them at the house with the back door open for a few weeks, at least until the work began. Twice every day Sharon came back across town to feed and walk them.

Eight weeks — and then 14 weeks — passed and work had still not begun on the house. Stanley and Jack became lonely and bored. Jack started howling at night and Stanley jumped into the neighbour's fishpond. More weeks and months went by. Sharon wondered if she should move Jack and Stanley, but she didn't know where they could go. Angus managed to arrange a one-month holiday for them with generous friends Kathy and Graham in Church Bay, which was a welcome respite.

After seven long months, Sharon and Angus were finally able to move back home and be reunited with Stanley and Jack. The dogs keep a close eye on the car now, making sure there are no plans to move again for a long, long time.

Asha

Asha, a five-year-old schnauzer cross, moved from Christchurch to Wellington on HUHA's second mercy mission to help animals escape the shaken city. Asha's family had had to move out of their red-zoned house and they hadn't been able to find another place where they could have Asha with them.

Although they loved her very much, they also knew Asha had been very stressed since the quakes and thought she would be better off out of Christchurch. They heard about the HUHA mission and, with heavy hearts, they went to meet the HUHA truck the following Saturday morning to give Asha away.

HUHA founder Carolyn took Asha's lead from her family, and she remembers a very sad moment as the daughter said a tearful goodbye. Carolyn promised her that Asha would be looked after for the rest of her life.

Asha first went to a foster carer in Wellington, but the woman worked during the day and it soon became clear that in her current stressed state Asha needed to be in a home where someone could be with her most of the time. So Ngaire, a HUHA volunteer who had another schnauzer and was home most days, agreed to foster Asha until a permanent family could be found. She helped make Asha feel at home and become less anxious.

One day while walking Asha on the beach, Ngaire met a family who

wanted to adopt Asha. She happily settled in with her new family for a year, but then a separation meant they could no longer keep her. For the third time, Asha had to find a new home.

This time Asha came to the HUHA shelter, where the staff were surprised to find that she was drinking excessively and peeing a lot inside. They did an array of tests on her but all were negative. The only likely conclusion was that Asha was still very stressed.

Asha became a favourite at the shelter, and she was showered with love and cuddles. She slowly began to relax.

One day some of the HUHA staff took Asha to a fair to represent HUHA, and a family came by who wanted to adopt her. Carolyn sat down with them and told them Asha's story. She explained how much stress the dog had been through, and that she would need a very caring and understanding home. The family listened carefully and decided to give Asha a chance.

At first, Asha was very anxious and would cling to new owner Adrienne's side. She would often pee on the floor. Slowly, however, Adrienne and her family gained Asha's trust and she began to relax. The peeing inside began to wane. Asha is now stress-free and enjoys daily walks on the beach with her new family and their cairn terrier Lochie.

Tetley

Five-year-old Tetley is a well-known personality around Lyttelton. Most people recognise the black Staffie-Labrador cross as he wanders about town on his own. The school children all know his name, as he strolls by at morning break and lunch to see if he might pick up any treats.

He has also been known to show up at a local watering hole called the Wunderbar. One night his owner Sarah got a call to say that she should come and pick him up, as some drunk girls were quite taken with him and were threatening to take him home.

Tetley has also always been very fond of his walks in the hills with Sarah and sometimes her father, Ian. Ever since Tetley was a pup, Sarah had taken him most days up into the hills to explore the many tracks above the harbour. Sometimes Sarah and Ian would take Tetley along on longer tramps in the Southern Alps.

On 22 February 2011, Tetley and Sarah were on the second floor of a friend's wooden townhouse in Lyttelton. As the house shook violently, Tetley ran downstairs and took cover in the bathroom. Sarah had to coax him outside.

One of Sarah's first thoughts was of Ian, as she knew that on Tuesdays he was usually out walking in the hills. He wasn't there when she got to their house, so she decided to go to look for him. She wasn't too worried, as he was an experienced tramper,

but she grabbed a flask of whisky just in case, along with some bandanas, Band-Aids, water and an extra jersey.

Sarah and Tetley headed up the Major Hornbrook track. They could soon see that the entire bluff above the track had fallen away, wiping out the track below. Rocks were falling from above them, shattering into pieces as they fell. Both Tetley and Sarah were nervous, but they continued, skidding down muddy banks and back up newly formed slips. Sarah knew this track well and it usually took about an hour to make it to the top. This day it took them almost three.

Since the track had largely disappeared, Tetley led them by scent. They made it to the top of the Bridle Path and then continued for another hour towards the Stan Helms track. As they were walking down this track,

Tetley began to bark and ran into a deep gully. It was there they found Sarah's father's body.

Sarah and Tetley sat with Ian for several hours before her brother-in-law and a family friend found them. It was cold and raining and dark slowly settled, as boulders like the one which had killed Ian continued to rain down around them. When three soldiers finally came to help carry out Ian's body, Tetley became very territorial and Sarah had to convince him to let them take her father away.

Two years after the big quake, Sarah and Tetley still go walking in the hills, and recently they went back to the site where they found Ian. The track down into the gully had become overgrown with weeds and Sarah might have missed it if Tetley hadn't alerted her to the faint path.

Molly

Molly, a little dog with a big attitude, has been accompanying Sue to the rest home that she manages for the past 13 years. The elderly Brussels griffon can usually be found either on or under Sue's desk, where she provides a nice distraction for the residents, who frequently stop to chat with her.

Molly used to sneak into the dining room after meal times and scrounge fallen scraps from under the tables. However, in the past few years she has become intolerant to many different foods, so now needs a strict diet of boiled chicken and rice.

The week before the 22 February 2011 earthquake, Molly became restless and tried to run away several times. At night, she kept waking up and scratching at the bedroom door to be let out. Once outside, she would sniff the air and search the garden. When Sue let her back inside, she would stay in bed only for a short time before she wanted to be let outside again.

When the big quake hit, Sue and Molly were in their office at the rest home. Sue immediately ran out of the office to check on the residents, who were still sitting in the dining room after lunch. After checking the staff were also OK and encouraging the residents to stay seated so they wouldn't get hurt during the continuing aftershocks, Sue's thoughts turned to Molly. She found that Molly had managed to get out of the office

despite the piles of fallen files, books and cabinets. Meanwhile, liquefaction was pouring into one of the wings and Sue and her staff had to lay duvets on the corridor floor to stem the flooding.

Just then the Wizard of Christchurch, who lives across the street from the rest home, called in to offer assistance and the use of his artesian well. Sue mentioned to him that Molly was missing and asked if he could keep an eye out for her. As he returned down the long, flooded driveway, the Wizard happened to glimpse a very wet and frightened dog behind the side gate. Molly was up to her neck in water and was very pleased to be rescued.

Sue and Molly lived at the rest home for the next three weeks to assist the staff and residents. After three days, they ventured out to collect dog food and a change of clothes from home. What was normally a 10-minute trip home turned into a three-hour return journey.

Molly is now nearly 14 and mainly ignores aftershocks. However, before any large quake hits, Molly resumes her old behaviour of waking at night and checking the garden, and Sue knows another shake is about to strike.

Molly was up to her neck in water and was very pleased to be rescued.

Jess

Jess is a seven-year-old German shepherd that has been working with police officer Shane in Auckland since she was just one year old. Born in Dunedin, Jess had a wind chime in her kennel as a pup to keep her from getting bored. She learned to watch the shadows and reflections as the chime danced in the sunlight.

This habit stuck with Jess and eventually meant that she couldn't be a front-line dog, because working at night with torches would distract her. However, Jess was excellent at victim recovery. She was deployed to the Melbourne bush fires in 2009 and to Samoa after the tsunami later that same year.

When the 22 February 2011 quake struck, Jess and the other three certified victim-recovery dogs at the Auckland police-dog unit were called upon to get to Christchurch as soon as possible. Jess with Shane, Chopper with Colin, Quake with Dan and Quanto with Chris prepared to leave as quickly as they could.

When the team arrived at the Christchurch airport, a woman who had just come from Australia came up to them and offered them a brown paper bag. 'You'll need this more than I do,' she said. Inside was a bottle of Bundaberg rum.

Driving from the airport through the northern suburbs, the team was relieved that there didn't appear to be too much damage. However, once they reached the CBD, it was much worse

than they could have imagined. Shane recalls it looked like a movie set just after the actors had finished for the day. Tables in restaurants were still neatly set with half-eaten meals on the plates. Tills were open and banks were abandoned unlocked. Shane and Colin say they will always remember the sound of the office alarms slowly winding down as their batteries died.

At first the police teams were working from 6 a.m. until 10 p.m., with one pair then on call each night. They searched many areas, such as the cathedral and the Grand Chancellor Hotel, that were soon afterwards declared unsafe for anyone to enter.

On one such search at the cathedral, Jess barked to indicate a victim twice at an area of rubble near the tower. Search teams combed the area and found no human victims, but they did find an injured pigeon that they later named Barney Rubble. Barney became a symbol of hope for the battered city. He was nursed back to health and eventually released back into the wild.

Another particularly harrowing search was a callout to the Forsyth Barr building, where the stairwell had collapsed. The team had to tie a rope to Chopper and hoist her up, limbs flailing, into a broken window.

Initially the police team had no safety gear and wore only flimsy plastic hard-hats which would have cracked if anything had landed on them. Eventually these were replaced with helmets so heavy that they had sore necks after five minutes of wearing them.

The police dogs also had special safety equipment. Since they weren't trained to work on broken concrete and rubble, they wore special Kevlar booties, which were ordered from Germany at a cost of $120 per set. The dogs would hop awkwardly in their boots until they got used to the sensation. Sometimes grit and dirt would get into them and rub on their paws until they became sore, but the boots kept them safe from cuts from the glass, wire and concrete shards.

In total, Jess and the other police dogs did 120 searches, poking into places that they normally wouldn't go. After two weeks, Jess's work was finished and she returned to Auckland to resume her normal life at the police station.

Jonah

Jonah was given to Mary as a birthday present 10 years ago by her mother, who bred and showed dachshunds for 50 years. His proper kennel name is 'Windy Corner All Black', so Jonah seemed a natural pet name in honour of the famous rugby winger.

Jonah was a New Zealand show champion by the time he was one year old, but in his spare time his true love is going to Halswell Quarry to hunt rabbits. He also loves the sea and will wade out into the waves until the water is far above his head, even though his short legs don't paddle very well. He is the alpha dog of the household and is well known for sending his brother Mertz in first to check on any uncertain situation.

Just before the 22 February 2011 quake, Mary discovered a lump in Jonah's throat. They were on holiday when the test results came back, showing that Jonah had thyroid carcinoma. They decided to return home early so that the surgery could be done on the Tuesday.

On the day of the surgery, Mary took the day off work so she could take Jonah into Total Vets at 7.30 a.m. At 12.30 p.m., she rang to find out how things were going. She was told that Jonah was just going in for surgery. She sat down to eat her lunch, then the quake struck.

Mary's first thought when the shaking had finished was that Jonah

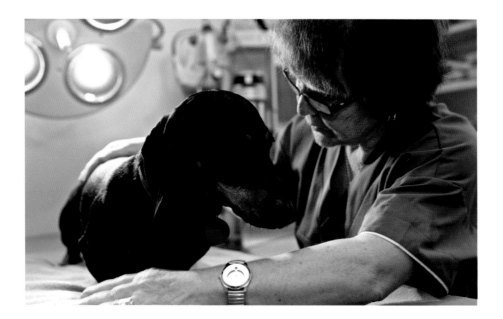

must be gone. She could not imagine how he could have survived surgery during such explosive shaking.

Jonah was under anaesthetic and vet Kirstin was halfway through his surgery when the quake hit. Surgical equipment flew off the shelves and out of the cupboards. The power instantly went off and all of the machines shut down, including the oxygen concentrator that was allowing Jonah to breathe. Kirstin had to blow air through a tube to keep him breathing until Amber, the vet nurse, could connect an oxygen bottle manually.

For 45 minutes, they chased the surgical table around the room as aftershocks hit, not willing to give up the delicate operation. Kirstin looked out of the window and watched as the fence collapsed, but she was so focused on Jonah's operation that she didn't grasp the severity of the situation.

When Jonah woke up after the operation, he was oblivious to the drama that had just unfolded. Mary managed to get a call through to the clinic about 4.30 p.m. and was told he was fine, but it was impossible for her to make it to the clinic to pick up Jonah. They agreed he would stay in the clinic overnight, alongside the eight other unfortunate cats and dogs that were in-patients that day. It must have been a dark and harrowing night for Jonah in his crate as the almost continuous aftershocks rocked and rolled.

Amber and Kirstin were back at the clinic just after first light the next morning to greet Jonah and their other patients, and Mary was able to pick him up later that morning. It took 18 months for Jonah to get his normal bark back, but he is now free of cancer and remains completely unaware of the remarkable way in which he survived the quake.

Tommy

Tommy, a border collie–fox terrier cross, came to Kirsti from the Aviation Security Service (Avsec), which had rescued him from the Pukekohe pound. Avsec had decided he was too boisterous and highly strung for their line of work, but they thought he could be well suited to search and rescue.

Kirsti found Tommy was a breeze to train as a USAR dog, because of his enthusiasm and his natural instincts. He would wiggle out of Kirsti's arms and bark when it was time for a search. The only challenge was finding a place to store his toys, since he soon learned how to snatch them off the top of the fridge or out of the cupboards by opening the doors.

Tommy was qualified as a USAR dog in November 2010, just three months before the 22 February quake. When he and Kirsti were called to duty, his greatest skill was searching the little spaces and holes, since at only 15 kilograms he was the smallest USAR dog in Christchurch at the time. His size also enabled Kirsti to carry him over dangerous areas that had lots of glass or sharp edges.

Tommy's other strength was that he was comfortable in a harness. During one search, Kirsti and Tommy abseiled off a roof onto the second floor of a building. Once their search was complete, the only way Tommy could get down was for him to be lowered to the ground on a

harness. Tommy cooperated with no hesitation.

Along with the other active Auckland USAR team, Sara and her dog Sasha (see page 176), Tommy and Kirsti were on night shifts, and they slept during the day at the tent camp in Latimer Square. None of them got much sleep. Kirsti and Sara bedded down between the dog crates that lined the tent. The dogs were restless and constantly moved in their cages. On top of that, the site was very busy, with people always coming and going.

Despite the sleep deprivation, Tommy did excellent work for 10 days until one day, when he was playing fetch with one of the technicians during his time off, he got the stick stuck in the back of his mouth. He was rushed to the cordon to the Veterinary Emergency Response Team (VERT). He stayed that night at the vet clinic, while Kirsti returned on her own to their tent. The next day Tommy was released, but a strong wind was whipping up dust and silt in thick clouds and the vets were worried that Tommy might get an infection. Later that day, Tommy and Kirsti flew back to Auckland.

In 2012, Kirsti and Tommy moved to Dunedin, and, with the closest USAR base four hours away, Tommy had to retire at the ripe young age of just four. He stays active with Rally-O (a dog sport based on obedience) and agility training, but most of his days are now spent lying on his back in the sun and swimming in the sea.

His greatest skill was searching the little spaces and holes, since at only 15 kilograms he was the smallest USAR dog in Christchurch at the time.

Quinn, Lia & Sky

Donna has had seven standard poodles over the past 20 years, and her current pack includes two-year-old Quinn, three-year-old Sky and six-year-old Lia. Lia and Sky are New Zealand show champions, and Quinn is currently training for his turn in the limelight.

Their elaborate hairdos take Donna 10 hours each to create. In their spare time, the dogs also love walks and having a picnic at the beach or the river.

When the September 2010 quake hit, Donna, Lia and Sky were fast asleep at their home in Kairaki Beach near Kaiapoi. Sky was in her crate under the stairway, so she was safe and remained fairly calm. Lia, on the other hand, had seven three-week-old pups that were with her in the whelping pen in the spare room. Objects hurtled around them, but fortunately nothing fell into the pen.

The pups' eyesight and hearing were just starting to develop when the September quake hit, and as they didn't know a world without aftershocks, they didn't seem to mind the shaking. Donna joked that she could sell them as 'quake-proof pups'. However, Lia was more greatly affected. Every time an aftershock struck, a look of terror would spread across her face and she would begin to shudder. Sky also became introverted and quiet.

Donna was concerned about

Sky and especially Lia, and when Auckland-raised Quinn joined her pack, she wondered how he would adjust. She had to find a way to keep all three of them from being stressed by the ongoing aftershocks.

It occurred to Donna that the dogs always looked to her when an earthquake hit, to see how she would react. She noticed that the more frightened she seemed, the more concerned the dogs would be. She decided to use the poodles' intelligence to her advantage. She would 'stand firm' and not let the dogs see when she was frightened.

From then on, every time there was a shake, Donna trained the dogs to come to her and play with their toys.

She would then laugh and clap and jump in the air to show the dogs she wasn't scared — which also helped to pull herself out of the fear she was actually feeling.

One time when a very small quake struck, Quinn came around the corner with his favourite ball in his mouth, ready to play. Donna laughed even harder, and his goofiness lightened everyone's mood.

It was not easy for Donna to laugh and play when inside she was shaking with fear, but the positive reinforcement worked. Quinn, Lia and Sky now think quakes are great fun and they run to find their toys each time the shaking begins.

Milo

When the 4 September 2010 earthquake struck, Milo, a beagle-fox terrier-basenji cross, was home alone in an upstairs apartment. His owner, Annie, was away for the night and could not get back to him until after daybreak that morning.

When she finally got home, Annie found the neighbour's chimney had fallen across the shared drive, and she had to scramble over the shattered bricks to reach the front door. She climbed the stairs and found that fallen pots, pans and kitchen appliances were blocking the door from the inside. She managed to push some of it aside and wedge the door open a crack. Milo sprinted frantically through the small gap, hyperventilating and with the whites of his eyes showing.

He ran down the steps and to the far corner of the garden, where he hid by the fence. Annie scooped him into her arms but, still shaking violently, he turned his head away from her as if to say, 'You weren't here; you let me down.'

After that, Milo wouldn't look Annie in the eyes and he refused to go back into the flat. He was so anxious that Annie took him to the vet, who prescribed the anti-anxiety drug Xanax. This helped to calm his nerves, but he still refused to go home. He stayed with Annie's friends for three months.

Annie would bring him back to the apartment every now and then, trying to coax him into going back inside. Milo would just press himself against the fence in the garden and refuse to go any further. Gradually, though, he got more and more used to coming back home, until finally one day he hesitantly agreed to come back inside.

Annie tried to divert his attention by giving him treats and a tennis ball. She closed the door for brief periods of time, until Milo finally relaxed enough to stay inside and not try to escape.

He was still very jumpy, and refused to be left alone. Annie had a dog door installed so that he could get outside whenever he wanted. She also attended a special workshop on Tellington TTouch therapy, which can be used to ease dogs' fear and anxiety. She learned to massage Milo's sides, squeeze his legs and rub his gums.

Slowly Milo's anxiety began to ease, and he made 'earthquake buddies' with other dogs that had been affected by the quakes. One of them, who was also home alone when the February earthquake struck, now comes to stay when her owner is busy. Just like Milo, she doesn't like to be left on her own.

Milo and his earthquake buddies hang out once a week and make each other feel more secure. They go out as a pack on adventures to the beach, Hagley Park and Bottle Lake Forest. One of these buddies, Jenny (see page 230), recently had a special birthday party and Milo dressed up in his finest bow tie to celebrate.

Slowly Milo's anxiety began to ease, and he made 'earthquake buddies' with other dogs that had been affected by the quakes.

Jenny

After the 22 February 2011 earthquake, Jenny, a 10-year-old fox terrier–collie cross, was left behind by her family when they decided to leave Christchurch to get away from the quakes. They packed their bags for Australia and found Jenny another home.

Jenny was distraught. One day she escaped and tried to find her old family, but she became lost. After several weeks of wandering, she was picked up by Animal Control and taken to the pound in a very sorry state. The pound was full of earthquake-orphan dogs and, as Jenny was old and would be harder to re-home than many of the other dogs, the pound did the paperwork to have her put down.

At the time, the Disabled Animals Welfare Group (DAWG) was helping animals with mental-health issues caused by the earthquakes, and its coordinator, Alex, heard about Jenny. He went to the pound to see if she was still alive. Jenny was very downtrodden and seemed to have given up hope. She did not even look up at Alex when he stood in front of her cell.

Annie, a volunteer for DAWG, agreed to foster Jenny until they could find her a good home, which they soon did. However, just eight months later, Jenny became homeless once again when her new family had to move out of their house and could not find rental

accommodation that would allow dogs. Once again, Jenny went to live with Annie and pined for several days for her old owners. She became very dejected and seemed to have given up hope again.

At this stage, Annie decided that Jenny had been through enough, and agreed to adopt her. However, wanting to bond with an owner and being desperate to belong, Jenny was very jealous of Annie's other dog, Milo (see page 226), and started nipping at him. Annie knew that she'd have to find Jenny yet another home.

Fortune smiled on Jenny when Annie took her and Milo to the beach for the first time since the earthquakes, and they met Annie's friend Anna. Anna considered herself to be a cat person and had never had a dog before, but when she saw Jenny's sweet face, she fell in love with her. She agreed to have her for three days on trial to be sure Jenny would not terrorise her cat, Tui. When the cat seemed to tolerate Jenny, Anna decided she would keep the dog. Little by little, Jenny began to relax again. She started nuzzling Anna, looking her in the eyes and sleeping inside. Anna got Jenny a bed and a kennel, but she preferred to sleep in the hall, as close to Anna's bed as she could.

Jenny is now the perfect family dog and happily plays with Anna's eight-year-old son, even if it means getting the occasional impromptu haircut. She enjoys daily walks on the beach and weekend adventures away in the campervan. Anna and Jenny both know that this is now her home forever.

Fritz

Fritz is an energetic nine-year-old schnauzer whose favourite hobbies are chasing cats and rabbits and jumping fences. The local cat loves to goad him by sitting at the top of the pergola, watching as Fritz bounces on his hind legs, higher and higher but not quite high enough.

He may not ever reach the cat, but his bouncing can take him high enough to climb most fences, hooking his front legs over the top until he can slowly hoist over the rest of his body. Such escapades meant Fritz had been through a few homes by the time he arrived at Anna and Ben's seven years ago.

On 22 February 2011, Fritz was outside alone as 12 tonnes of liquefaction slowly oozed up into the front and back garden of his house in Edgeware, just north of the Christchuch CBD. It took many hours for Anna and Ben to make it home. He was so scared that he jumped the 1.8 metre high fence, and by the time Anna and Ben got home he was nowhere to be found.

Since they had no power and water and there was thick liquefaction everywhere, Anna and Ben couldn't stay in their house, but they continued to search the area for Fritz. The morning after the earthquake, Anna and Ben went to the pound and the SPCA, where large crowds of people were gathered, looking for their pets.

They put up signs around the

neighbourhood and surrounding areas, and soon started getting text messages from people who had spotted Fritz. A lady who lived about a kilometre from their house had picked him up and put him in her yard with her two dogs. She sent a text message to Anna to let her know she had Fritz, but he panicked during a big aftershock and ran away. By the time Anna and Ben got there, he was gone again.

For two more days, Ben and Anna followed the same routine: visit the pound, then the SPCA, then search all Fritz's favourite spots. But there was still no sign of their dog. Then finally, on the third day, they got a more solid lead. A woman in Ashburton rang to say they had found a dog that they thought might be Fritz.

Anna and Ben were dumbfounded. How had Fritz made it all the way to Ashburton?

As it turned out, Fritz was actually with the woman's daughter Katya, who lived very close to Anna and Ben. Katya hadn't been able to

contact the Christchurch SPCA, so she had asked her mum in Ashburton to ring the Timaru SPCA, who gave her Anna and Ben's details from the SPCA lost animals database.

Katya had tried walking Fritz around the neighbourhood to see if he could find his way home, but they couldn't get down Anna and Ben's road because of the silt. She had no power or water, and although everyone else had left the neighbourhood, she didn't want to leave Fritz. She locked her cat in the garage, put her own dog on the floor and invited her esteemed guest to sleep on her bed.

When Anna and Ben went to pick up Fritz from Katya's house, it took an hour to corner him because he was so scared. Although he is normally quite placid and sweet, he growled and snapped.

Once they got him home, he soon settled in and was back to jumping fences and chasing the cat, but he wouldn't let Anna and Ben out of his sight for days.

Buk & Que

Linda adopted Buk, a German shepherd–cattle dog cross, and Que, a collie–Labrador cross, from the Christchurch pound, confident that they had the requisite drive and determination to start search and rescue training.

Que was six months old when he arrived at the pound in 2006, and he was well on his way through his USAR training when Buk arrived there as a one-year-old in 2008.

Buk and Que have completely opposite personalities but they are the best of mates. Que is a clown, throwing his head back when he barks and making everyone laugh by getting himself into silly situations. He has a very expressive face, so Linda always knows what he is thinking.

As for Buk, he started out as a frustrated and angry young dog.

USAR work has helped him to focus that frustration, and his very serious and determined nature is now his strength in USAR work.

On 22 February 2011, Linda was working in the city when the quake hit. She immediately raced home on her bike to pick up Buk and Que, her gear and her truck, then headed back into the CBD. For over 30 hours straight, they cleared buildings by checking that no one was trapped inside. They didn't take a break until 4.30 a.m. on 23 February, when they finally met

up with the other USAR teams and were advised to get some sleep.

In the wee hours of the morning, the handlers and dogs all went back to USAR handler Janelle's house for the most bizarre slumber party they'd ever had. Six handlers were lined up in sleeping bags on the floor, with the dogs all parked in the drive outside.

The team slept for just an hour and a half, then at first light they were straight back into the city again. Linda, Buk and Que helped at many important searches around the city, including at the PGC building, the cathedral and the CTV building.

Linda describes those first days as surreal. She, Buk and Que went on autopilot, doing the things they had done in training twice each week, every week, for years. For the most part, Buk and Que did their job without hesitation. They would go into buildings where Linda couldn't follow to search, climb ladders or planks and go under and through tight spaces, all to make sure no one was trapped inside the buildings.

But some situations were too much even for them. At one building that had 'pancaked', Buk navigated the ladder onto the twisted steel and concrete of what had been a three-storey building. It was a horrible site to be searching, full of tight spaces and sharp edges. Buk was completely focused on his search, but when it was time to come back down, he baulked. The ladder seemed to appear from a black hole and Buk refused to go down into that void. Linda and another USAR handler, Tim, ended up carrying him down the ladder.

Buk and Que's confidence and independence in searching highlighted the importance of their training and preparation. Night training, 72-hour exercises, agility and directional training, climbing ladders or planks, working in small spaces and working among people, noises and distractions were all critical aspects that helped them perform so expertly in the wake of such a huge disaster, which no one ever expected would happen right on their own doorstep.

Tezza

In June 2011, Jacqui made one of the hardest phone calls she had ever had to make. She rang Dogwatch and told them that she needed to give her best friend, Tezza, up for adoption.

She said that she had to do what was best for the five-year-old Australian cattle dog–Staffie cross, and she didn't feel it was fair to keep her in Christchurch any longer. Tezza was so stressed by the earthquake activity that every time a truck drove by, she would jump into Jacqui's lap. Tezza's hair was falling out and she had bald patches under her legs and on her chest.

Dogwatch told Jacqui that on 25 June, HUHA was taking 24 dogs that needed to get out of Christchurch up to Wellington to find new homes,

and that maybe Tezza could be one of them. When Jacqui dropped off Tezza at the HUHA truck and signed her away, the HUHA team could see how much she loved the dog. They both looked very scared.

Tezza and Jacqui's heart-wrenching goodbye made the television news, so by the time Tezza got to Wellington she had already created a lot of interest. Macaela and Nathan had offered to foster Tezza, and expected to pick her up when the HUHA truck arrived in Wellington. However, another couple offered to

give Tezza a permanent home, so she went with them.

Unfortunately, this family had just lost a dog and it turned out that they just weren't ready to adopt a new one, so they soon returned Tezza to HUHA, who placed her in a foster home. This family had a young boxer who annoyed Tezza very much, and finding Tezza a new home became urgent. When HUHA volunteer Cherie found out that Tezza needed a new home — her third in the few months since she had arrived in Wellington — she remembered that Macaela and Nathan had really wanted to foster Tezza when she first arrived.

Cherie rang them and, much to her relief, Macaela and Nathan were very keen to foster Tezza. After just two weeks, they decided they could never let her go.

At first, Tezza was very cautious and would yelp if people came too close or if she was startled. She didn't mind being left alone in the house, but would get very concerned when other people were around and she lost sight of Macaela and Nathan. Sometimes, she would jump out of open windows and over fences to chase them if they left.

Most of Tezza's hair has now grown back, although it is still like peach fuzz in places, so Macaela's mum has knitted her a few jerseys to keep her warm. She is also now a much friendlier and calmer dog. She loves to sit on Nathan's or Macaela's lap, snuggle up to their necks and fall asleep. She also now sleeps under the blankets in bed with them.

Tezza loves socialising with other dogs on the beach, and chasing and biting the waves. She's recently started to swim without being coaxed, and is gaining confidence every day.

Awhi & Echo

Awhi, a 16-year-old terrier–dachshund cross, is a pound dog from Napier. Although bossy and feisty, she was an anxious and timid dog even before the quakes, and she hates water bottles, remote controls and the wind.

Echo, an 11-year-old Labrador, was a breeding dog before coming to live with Philip and Sian. Her primary passion is food, but she also loves duck hunting with Philip and making Philip and Sian laugh with her silly pranks.

Awhi and Echo are very close and hate being separated. It was therefore unfortunate that when the 22 February 2011 quake struck, Awhi was inside sheltering from the rain while Echo was outside in the garden. After the roar of the quake subsided, they could hear each other but they were trapped apart.

Meanwhile, Sian was working in the central city. When the shaking finally stopped, one of her first thoughts was of Awhi and Echo, especially when she heard that the quake was centred near their home in Mt Pleasant. She caught a ride home with a friend on his motorbike, which enabled them to dodge much of the heavy traffic. They arrived home in less than an hour.

Sian walked up the steep drive to their house and saw that all of the windows had blown out and most of

the bricks had fallen off. When she opened the door, the entire house had been flooded by the broken hot-water cylinder. Not one item was left in a cupboard or drawer, and the gas heater had been ripped off the wall. Awhi and Echo were nowhere in sight.

Sian began to panic, but a few minutes later, Awhi tiptoed down the hall. She was terrified and tried to crawl up Sian's legs. Sian grabbed her and went to the gate leading to the garden, where she had left Echo that morning. A dusty, bright orange figure came stumbling out from amid a pile of fallen bricks. Awhi whimpered at the site of Echo, frantically licking her dusty coat to make sure she was OK. Echo nuzzled her back.

Sian grabbed both dogs and a few essentials and walked to a neighbour's house. Although it was just metres up the road, the house was almost untouched, but their two dogs were also very frightened. The neighbours got some bones from the freezer and everyone moved to the garden to weather the many aftershocks. Awhi was still terrified, but Echo was completely content to chew on her bone.

That night, Awhi and Echo slept with Sian and Philip in a tent in the neighbour's garden. Awhi shook with fear all night. Echo was so sore from bruising that she couldn't sleep. She whimpered all night as the others managed small doses of sleep between the many aftershocks.

The first few times that Sian and Philip went back to their house to clean up the gigantic mess, Awhi refused to go back inside. Gradually she mustered up the courage to re-enter. The house was badly damaged but it was structurally sound and habitable.

Eighteen months later, Sian, Philip, Awhi and Echo had to move out for three months while their house was repaired, and Echo and Awhi had to move three times during that period. However, the repairs are now near completion, and Awhi and Echo are enjoying getting back into their old routines.

After the roar of the quake subsided, they could hear each other but they were trapped apart.

Poppy

Nine-year-old Rottweiler Poppy has always been an inside dog, but on 22 February 2011 she was outside on the balcony 'babysitting' three-month-old Australian terrier Eric while their owners Katrina and Richard were at work. Poppy didn't mind being outside too much, since Eric would curl up with her on her bed and keep her nice and warm.

When the quake struck, Katrina was at a seminar in the Hagley Park netball stadium. It took her several hours to make her way home to Huntsbury, south of the city on the Port Hills, and she arrived at the same time as her son, Sam. Their neighbours told them that the house was too dangerous to enter, so Sam and the neighbour's son carefully picked their way around the outside of the house to the balcony to try to find Poppy and Eric. It looked like a bomb had exploded, with bricks torn from the house and scattered around the balcony and garden. They found Eric hiding under a broken plant pot, but Poppy was nowhere to be seen.

Katrina and Richard spent hours calling for Poppy around the neighbourhood. They put up missing posters and visited all of the places she used to walk. They had to move out of their house for three days, but they kept coming back in case Poppy returned home.

On the third day, a neighbour came running over with a transistor radio and told Katrina that he just heard someone who had found a lost

Rottweiler. He had told the station to have the caller try the name Mrs Poppy, as Katrina often called her, and the dog had responded. Katrina immediately called the radio station, who connected her with city councillor Sue Wells. Sue had found the Rottweiler the day of the quake and taken her to her house in Opawa — just down the hill from Poppy's home. Poppy had since been living a life of luxury, schmoozing with other city councillors and sleeping on Sue's bed.

When Katrina went to pick up Poppy, Sue recounted the story of how she had found the dog. After the quake, Sue had been heading into the city with her border collie Pepper to collect her children from school, when two backpackers approached her. They had found Poppy wandering on the corner of Fitzgerald and Cashel streets. They tied a belt around her collar to use as a lead, but they weren't sure what to do with her. Sue, being an animal lover, agreed to take her home and try to find her family.

As Katrina heard this story, her mouth fell open in disbelief. Katrina worked in an office on Cashel Street, and for two weeks prior to the quake, Richard had been picking Katrina up from work because one of their cars was in the shop. They always met at the corner of Fitzgerald and Cashel streets, and then they would take Poppy out to Bottle Lake Forest for a run. Poppy must have remembered this meeting place, and so when the quake struck, she ran 7 kilometres to that very spot, hoping that she would find Katrina there waiting.

Keisha, Robbie, Lance & Layla

Late in the evening of 3 September 2010, then five-year-old border collie Keisha went into labour. She gave birth to two pups, Richie and Toby, just before midnight. The third puppy, Lance, came a couple of hours later, and then at 4 a.m. the last pup, Layla, was born.

Ann was cleaning up the newspapers around the four newborn pups when she suddenly heard the pups' father, Robbie, barking outside. This was unusual behaviour, especially in the middle of the night, and Ann yelled out at him in irritation. Moments later, just 35 minutes after Layla was born, the big quake struck.

The power instantly went out and Ann remembers the sound of glass breaking and everything falling around her. Luckily nothing fell on Keisha and the pups, but the house around them was severely damaged.

As soon as it was daylight, Ann inspected it more closely. She lifted up the carpet in her bedroom and found she could see straight through to the ground underneath. One entire wall of her bedroom had opened up to the garage, part of the house had dropped and many big cracks had appeared.

Since Ann's bedroom lay in ruins, she moved into the room where Keisha and her pups slept. She took the doors off the wardrobe and slept inside it for the next three nights. Although Ann was traumatised, the dogs were quite calm and seemed

unaffected by the quake.

After three days, Ann decided to leave Christchurch as she had no power or water and she was having difficulty keeping the pups warm without any heating. She piled her five dogs and four puppies into the campervan and headed to her sister's house in Kaikoura, where they stayed for two weeks. After this, they were offered temporary accommodation in the city outskirts, where Ann and the dogs stayed until Christmas. Ann re-homed two of the pups, but she couldn't decide whether Lance or Layla would be better for showing, so she ended up keeping them both.

Just before Christmas, power was restored at their house, so even though it was still uninhabitable, Ann and her dogs moved back home, sleeping in the campervan in the yard and using the facilities for cooking and cleaning.

In early February 2011, Ann had to have one of her elderly dogs put down and on 22 February, she had just been to collect the dog's ashes when the region's second big quake struck. As her van rocked violently on top of the Moorhouse Avenue overpass, Ann prayed that it wouldn't collapse, while the dogs barked anxiously in the back.

Ann managed to drive as far as the Avon River, but they couldn't get any further because the bridge had been closed. She couldn't walk the six dogs she had with her all the way home on her own, so she sat in the van and waited for two hours until her son could get there. They then each took three dogs and headed home on foot.

That night Ann packed up her things, coaxed the dogs into the campervan and drove down to Ashburton to stay with friends. The move south became permanent when the house she had lived in for 28 years was red-zoned. Keisha, Robbie, Lance, Layla and another of Robbie's daughters, Heidi, love their new home. Lance and Layla are now New Zealand show champions, just like their parents.

Oscar

Not long after the 22 February 2011 earthquake, Ian was reading his email when a message from the Selwyn Dog Training Club caught his eye: 'Wanted: Home for an abandoned, old, large golden retriever. Age unknown'.

Ian and his wife had been doing what they could to help abandoned dogs, and they were prepared to adopt at least one. This poor old fellow seemed a good candidate. Ian telephoned the next day and arranged a visit to the outskirts of the broken city.

Oscar's background was confusing, but Ian pieced together that he had been abandoned twice. After the 4 September 2010 quake, he was abandoned near Rangiora and had been pushed onto another family that could not really look after him. After the 22 February 2011 quake, he was abandoned again. His next owner found him filthy, beaten, scavenging and wandering the streets. They were now moving to Australia and so Oscar had to find a new home yet again.

When Ian first visited Oscar, he was enclosed with several other noisy dogs in a small, badly kept yard. All of the dogs crowded fearlessly around Ian except for Oscar. From a distance, Oscar's ribs showed beneath his dirty, matted coat. His tail was damaged and his left eye was sunken from a recent blow. He was eating bits of cardboard and old rags.

Ian softly called to Oscar, offering a treat in the palm of his outstretched hand. Oscar hesitated, then slowly came forward and timidly grabbed the treat. Ian decided then and there to adopt him.

Ian returned the next day with his two dogs, Bess and Tinker, to pick up Oscar. When Ian opened the van door, Oscar scrambled in with the other dogs without hesitation.

The vet believed Oscar was at least eight years old and confirmed that he was grossly underweight. Over the next few days, Ian began learning more about Oscar's tastes. He discovered that Oscar loved bananas and jam. He offered Oscar a cozy basket in which to snuggle, but found that he preferred to lie on an old rug with his head between his sprawled-out front legs.

Ian also gathered more clues about Oscar's past. At the dog park, Oscar stumbled across the open grassy park, his long back legs wobbling as if he had spent months confined in a small space. He knew the commands of sit, down, heel and wait, so he had been well trained at some stage. Most peculiarly, whenever he saw a woman riding a bicycle he became agitated, chasing the cyclist and barking frantically.

Two years on, Oscar has a thick, shiny coat. His weight has increased, but he still has wobbly back legs and arthritis makes it difficult for him to stand or even sit up for long periods. His sunken eye weeps constantly. He is gentle and well-behaved, but is still nervous and fearful of humans, and he never strays far from Ian. A slamming door brings fear to his eyes, and an unintentional raised hand makes him cringe. However, he is one of the lucky earthquake orphans to find a family that will continue to offer him affection and care for the rest of his days.

Charlie

Charlie is a three-year-old Jack Russell-papillon cross that had an inauspicious start in life but has proven that she is a survivor. Her mother, a long-haired Jack Russell, was walking in the park one day with her owner, Jack, when a male papillon attacked her.

Jack couldn't get the papillon off and, fearing the worst, he took his dog to the vet for the canine equivalent of the morning-after pill. Despite the precaution, two months later Charlie was born, the only pup in the litter.

When Charlie was 10 weeks old, Karen adopted her from Jack. She was a very laidback dog and even tolerated Tomas the cat licking her ears. Her favourite things were going on holidays with her family in their pop-top campervan and walking on the beach — as long as she didn't get wet.

As it was for so many Christchurch dogs, 22 February 2011 was a life-changing day for wee Charlie. She was home alone when the quake hit, and objects and furniture tumbled around her. When the shaking finally stopped she managed to escape out the cat door, and by the time Karen got home she was waiting in the drive with a terrified look on her face.

After the quake, Charlie began sleeping on Karen's bed. Karen noticed that she had developed an uncanny ability to predict when an aftershock was coming. Just

before the shaking would start, Charlie would make her own unique earthquake warning signal, a guttural growl that started soft and reached a crescendo as the quake grew nearer. She would then go outside and sniff the air, as if she could sense which direction it was coming from and try to growl it away.

Karen had never heard Charlie make this noise before the February quake, but she soon found that her signal was correct every single time. Charlie could even predict tiny shakes that Karen couldn't feel. Whenever Charlie made her special noise, Karen would look on the internet to see if an aftershock had been recorded. One always had.

Perhaps because of her special ability to sense when quakes are coming, Charlie's temperament has changed. She is now nervous and timid and acts as though she is constantly on guard. Her appetite has changed as well; she refuses to eat the dried dog food she always ate before the earthquakes, and will now eat only human food, sitting beside the dinner table and eating with the rest of the family.

Charlie particularly doesn't like to be left at home alone, and sharp noises or raised voices frighten her. This can make it difficult when the Crusaders play, as Karen and her partner can't help but scream and yell as they cheer the home team on.

Boo

Boo is a four-year-old Labrador–bull terrier cross that arrived at the pound when she was just one year old. On her first day there, she jumped the pound fence. When Brenda, the pound manager and national trainer for USAR dogs, went looking for her, she saw four white legs sticking out of a chicken coop.

Brenda feared the worst, but found Boo fast asleep with the chooks pecking calmly around her.

The next day, Boo jumped three 1.8 metre fences in order to get to Brenda's house. Brenda knew then that she was USAR material, and handed her on to handler Tim to begin her training. Boo passed her first operational assessment after only six months of training. Tim named her Boo not only because it is the acronym for Base of Operations, the hub of any USAR deployment, but also because her white coat makes her look as though she's seen a ghost.

This is apt since, when Boo is at home, she is afraid of a number of things. She runs away whenever there is a loud noise or a rubbish truck, or if Tim picks up a hose or the vacuum cleaner. Most of all, Boo is afraid of earthquakes. After the 4 September 2010 quake, Boo adopted a space between the couch and the La-Z-Boy as a bunker during aftershocks.

But despite this fear, as soon as Boo gets into her crate in the back of the car and her search toy is pulled out, her eyes go black and a switch flicks

inside her. Suddenly, she is in search mode and nothing can hold her back from completing her searching task.

When the 22 February 2011 quake hit, Boo was in her crate in the conservatory, and a large cupboard and a glass sliding door fell on top of her. When Tim got home soon afterwards, Boo was terrified.

After Tim had ensured his family were all safe, he and Boo headed into the city. One of their first searches was at the cathedral. As they were searching inside, a strong aftershock hit. The building was very unstable, with lots of loose rubble, and bricks started falling down around them. Tim decided there was no time to find Boo, but as he turned to sprint out, Boo brushed by him and was outside waiting when Tim emerged.

Tim and Boo worked for over 30 hours straight along with the rest of the USAR dogs and handlers. Towards the end of the shift, they were in the PGC building, climbing and crawling through multiple floors for over an hour. Tim could tell Boo was mentally and physically drained. They tried to sleep for several hours before they were back at work again.

For the next few weeks, Tim and Boo worked day shifts from first light until nine or ten o'clock at night. Together they completed over 30 searches within the Christchurch CBD and in Sumner. Like all USAR handlers, Tim was a volunteer, and so he had to take time off from his job at the city council's water and waste unit. Even when Tim and Boo's shifts finished, Tim was called to various meetings and inquests, and they remained on call in case of aftershocks.

Kenske

Kenske, or Ken as he is usually called, came to live with Mai and Ben when he was just eight weeks old. They expected him to grow into a huge black Labrador like his father Zeus, but he was still quite small by the time he was one year old and fully grown.

Ken is a master escape artist. He regularly sneaks through the hedge and follows his nose through neighbouring gardens in search of food or other friendly dogs. He loves playing with other dogs and, true to his breed, loves food even more. His naughtiest deed of all time was dragging an entire homemade cheesecake off the bench and scarfing it in less than five minutes. Later that night the cheesecake reappeared in a less appetising form, all over the carpet.

On 22 February 2011, Ken was alone in the garage of his house in St Martins, south of the CBD. When the earthquake struck, a heavy toolbox fell off a shelf towards Ken and, to escape, he dived into a glass door 4 millimetres thick. The glass shattered into sharp fragments, framing his escape route. Forcing his way through, he suffered a large cut beside his eye and several more on his paws and legs. Once outside he ran and hid in the bushes, anxiously waiting for a friendly face to appear.

Both Ben and Mai were at work, and Rory, a good friend who had

been staying with them, was able to get home first. He noticed the smashed glass then saw a bloodied and shaken Ken peering out of the bushes. He removed several shards of glass from Ken's various wounds and found some old clothes, which he used to create a makeshift bandage around Ken's head and leg. He then offered Ken a rare treat of some human comfort food, which Ken inhaled in true Labrador style.

Ben had been working in New Brighton and Mai in Sumner. It took roughly three hours for them both to walk and wade home through flooded Bexley and Ferrymead. Ken was ecstatic when they returned and limped down the drive to greet them. That night, as everyone bedded down in tents in the garden, Ken curled up next to Mai, growling as the tremors continued to ripple through the neighbourhood.

After the quake, Ken hated being left alone — and especially wouldn't be left in the garage. His wound healed into a permanent scar next to his eye. He would follow Mai around everywhere and bark loudly at every aftershock.

Eventually, as the aftershocks got smaller, his hackles would just go up and he accepted being left alone for longer and longer. His confidence continues to grow, and with Mai now pregnant, they are confident that Ken will make an excellent canine companion for their growing family.

Jess

Jess, a seven-year-old huntaway-Labrador cross, was home alone in Parklands in northeast Christchurch when the 22 February 2011 quake hit. When owner Kerrie made it home from work three and a half hours later, she discovered Jess had broken through the fence.

Kerrie found Jess wandering on New Brighton Road, covered in grey silt from the deep liquefaction through which she had waded on her way out of the back garden.

After the big quake, Jess and her family had to move out of their house for a month while emergency repairs were completed. Jess was very happy when they were finally able to move back home because Kerrie's parents, whose house had also been badly damaged, had rented the house next door. Kerrie's father spent most days at home.

Although Jess had never been a digger before, she began digging under the fence to go over to his house, rather than spend all day at home alone. Kerrie and her husband, Dean, couldn't stop her digging, so they eventually decided just to take the dog next door each day on the way to work.

On 13 June 2011, major aftershocks brought more liquefaction, this time even worse than in February. Grey streams literally flowed straight through Kerrie and Dean's house. The entire yard was covered in 30 centimetres of silt.

Once again Jess and her family had to move out. This time they moved in with Kerrie's parents, whose rented house right next door miraculously was not affected by liquefaction.

Eventually, Kerrie and Dean's house was red-zoned, and in October 2012 they moved into a new house in Burwood. Suddenly, Jess began digging again with a vengeance. She chose just one spot to dig under the fence, and every time Kerrie and Dean filled in the hole, she dug it out again. She wouldn't run away — Kerrie would find her on the other side of the fence, lying in the front garden or the driveway — she simply didn't like to be fenced in and left on her own.

Kerrie and Dean tried filling the hole with rocks and bricks, but Jess dug them out again, her paws becoming bloody and raw and her nose grazed. It never seemed to occur to Jess that she could dig under the fence in another place. They tried putting steel bars a metre into the ground and then filling the hole with bricks, but Jess bent the steel rods and still managed to dig her way out.

Finally, wooden beams under the steel bars then topped with bricks stopped her from escaping. However, once she could no longer dig her way out, Jess started breaking into the house through the cat flap. She would rip out the flap and chew on it until her gums bled. Twice she shattered the entire glass door in which the cat flap was embedded.

Eventually Kerrie and Dean had to replace the door with safety glass and remove the cat flap so Jess could come and go through the empty hole. They now leave Jess outside when they go to work, but she comes straight back inside as soon as they leave. In the afternoon, when she hears Kerrie's car returning, Jess runs through the garage and stands waiting in front of the house as if she's been there all along.

Whizz

When Whizz was eight weeks old, malamute breeders Ann and Clive sent her to live with a loving family in Blenheim. However, six years later the family rang Ann from their new home in the North Island to say that they could no longer keep her.

Ann and Clive took Whizz back without hesitation and, after an adventurous trip south, she was back to enjoy a wonderful life with them that included such sports as sled racing and weight pulling.

Whizz is now 13 years old and can no longer compete in sled racing, although she still enjoys a good swim in the river. She is going a little bit blind and has epilepsy, which is why she happened to be at a vet clinic in central Christchurch on 22 February 2011. She had been vomiting, which had made her epilepsy medicine less effective, so Clive dropped her off in the morning to have some routine tests.

Kirstin, the vet, rang late morning to let them know that the tests all looked normal and that they could pick up Whizz anytime. Ann and Clive sat down to have lunch before they drove into the city. Then the quake hit.

At Ann and Clive's house in Kaiapoi, the quake caused only moderate shaking, and with communications in the city out, they had no idea how badly the central city had been damaged. Clive set out to collect

Whizz, but after two hours of driving he was stopped by an army roadblock and forced to turn back. It took him another three hours to get home again.

By the time Clive got home, Ann had watched the news and knew how severe the quake had been. They had no idea what state the vet clinic or Whizz were in, so they made a second desperate attempt to reach the city together. Again they were turned back.

That night, Kirstin managed to ring them to let them know that Whizz was fine. She could spend the night with several other dogs and a cat at the clinic, although there was no power or water. The staff had washed the surgery down with water from the hydrotherapy pool and had given Whizz and the other patients distilled water from the medical equipment to drink.

The following morning, Ann made their third attempt to reach Whizz. She loaded the car with 40 litres of water for the clinic, and made a huge, circuitous loop around the city to avoid the roadblocks at the Avon River. It took many hours, but this time she made it all the way to the clinic.

She arrived before the clinic opened, but before long Kirstin cycled up and let Ann in. Whizz was happy to see Ann, although she had remained completely calm throughout the entire incident.

Ann and Whizz arrived home three and a half hours later, and Whizz has never had another seizure since.

Jeff

Huntaways Jeff and his brother Gee were born on a farm outside Christchurch just after the 4 September 2010 quake. They weren't the pick of the litter, and their future as working farm dogs didn't look hopeful.

Born on a different farm, they might have been shot there and then, but luckily this farmer saw things differently. He decided to try to find them a new home.

However, every Christchurch animal shelter was bulging with the animals that had been abandoned or had to be re-homed as people lost their houses to quake damage. There was simply no more room, and for many owners the only option was to put their pets to sleep.

The farmer considered this option too, but then he heard about the Wellington animal-rescue organisation called HUHA, which was organising a truck to take dogs affected by the earthquakes to the North Island to be re-homed. This would help relieve some of the pressure on the overstretched Christchurch shelters.

The HUHA team left Wellington at 8 p.m. on a Friday, crossing Cook Strait on the ferry then driving south all night to arrive in Christchurch first thing on Saturday morning. When the truck arrived in Christchurch, the farmer was waiting with many other

families and their dogs.

After the farmer had signed all of the paperwork, a HUHA volunteer picked up Jeff and Gee and put them into their crates in the truck. The next 24 hours would be a terrifying journey, but it would all be worth it, as a new life awaited them in Wellington.

The HUHA truck arrived at the Moa Point pound in Wellington early on a wet and cold Sunday morning. Nicole and Callum had planned to meet the truck when it arrived, but it took ages to get the children ready and in the car. By the time they reached Moa Point, many of the dogs had already been claimed.

As soon as they arrived, a HUHA volunteer thrust a dishevelled-looking dog towards them and told them to take him for a walk. The young dog looked like he was the last cab off the rank; he was dirty and forlorn. However, as they walked with him, Jeff's sweet nature began to shine

through his scruffy appearance.

It was a huge decision for Nicole and Callum, because they had never had a dog before and they didn't want to have to send him back if they made the wrong choice. However, they felt confident that Jeff would be a wonderful addition to their family.

It was a massive adjustment for Jeff to move from a farm into suburbia. He had never lived outside of a crate and at first he refused to come inside the house. He was very shy and didn't make a noise for the first week except to cry.

Slowly, though, Jeff got used to city life and decided his new home was quite acceptable. The couch was a much better bed than his crate, and the children could be herded around the garden as if they were lambs. He went running with Callum and riding in the car with Nicole. In fact, his new life in Wellington was everything a dog could have hoped for.

Keepa

Keepa, a six-year-old blue heeler–border collie cross, was brought to the Christchurch pound as a four-month-old pup. He had been tied up outside some shops all day and no one had come back for him.

When he got to the pound, he immediately jumped onto the table, and his future owner Brenda said, 'Wow, he's a keeper! Let's hope nobody comes for him.'

Luckily no one did, because Brenda went on to train Keepa as a USAR dog. On 22 February 2011, he was one of the first dogs on the scene of the collapsed CTV building. While working on the pile of rubble, glass and concrete, Keepa helped lead rescuers to several buried people before he cut his paw.

Although it was a small nick, it bled profusely. Brenda had two other dogs to look after, so she handed him to the nearest person to patch him up. Mike, who worked in the nearby IRD building and had come across to the CTV site to try to help, led Keepa away to find a bandage.

An hour or so later, Keepa returned with a bandage so big that it looked more like he had a broken leg than just a cut paw. But by the next search he was ready to go again. He couldn't wait to get back in there.

Keepa goes about his work quietly and very methodically. Brenda is

careful with Keepa, because if she raises her voice or reprimands him, his ears go down and he gives her a look as if to say, 'If you think you can do better, then go right ahead!'

One of the more unusual searches Keepa took part in was in a bakery at 2 a.m. It was full of the lovely smells of fresh mince pies and mashed potatoes. The temptations must have been unbearable, but Keepa remained in search mode, not even looking or sniffing the many treats all around him. However, on the way out, Keepa finally found something even a dog in search mode couldn't resist: a giant bowl of mashed potatoes and gravy. A quick 'leave' from Brenda was all it took, though, to put him back on task.

Keepa's strengths as a USAR dog are his agility (he can jump one and a half metres from a sitting position) and his methodical nature, which is why he was chosen to work at many of the most dangerous sites that day, squeezing through many small nooks and crannies. One such site was the Smith City car park building, where three parking levels had compacted into one small layer. Keepa and Brenda had to be tied to a fire truck ladder and hoisted onto the top of the building. By then it was drizzly, wet and starting to get dark. Keepa searched every car and confirmed that no one was trapped there.

Thorn

Thorn is a five-year-old chihuahua cross, who until the day of the 22 February 2011 earthquake had had a very happy life. His owner took him everywhere: to work during the day and to the pub afterwards.

But the day of the quake, everything changed for Thorn. His owner lost his job and felt he had no choice but to escape to Australia. After much agonising, he decided to leave Thorn behind. He gave the vet some money for Thorn's care, as the dog was suffering from stress and anxiety, and left him in what he thought were very capable hands with a neighbour and his landlady.

Unfortunately, it turned out that the neighbour and landlady just couldn't look after Thorn, and they took him to the vet to be put down.

Luckily, the vet knew what a special dog Thorn was and how much his previous owner had loved him. He refused to put him down and instead rang Dogwatch to see if they could find him a home. Thorn was placed in a foster home for three days, before his luckiest break yet. He was given one of just 26 spots on a special truck taking dogs north to Wellington to escape the shakes and find new homes.

On 25 June 2011, Thorn was loaded onto the HUHA truck along with the other dogs and puppies and an

assortment of other animals. The dogs were all put into crates, with a friend or sibling if they had one, and the crates were stacked on top of each other, with the puppies and small dogs on the top and the bigger dogs on the bottom. HUHA volunteers gave them all blankets and chew toys, and added Rescue Remedy to their water bowls to help calm them.

The truck drove the four hours to Picton and waited for the 2 a.m. ferry to Wellington. Once in the capital, they drove out to the Moa Point pound, where loving families were waiting to foster and adopt each of the Christchurch earthquake orphans.

When the truck arrived, Jim the driver pulled the door aside. Vari, one of the HUHA trustees, remembers a lump rising in her throat. Rather than the bouncy, happy pack she was expecting, a wall of confused and broken dogs stared out at her. Sally, who had already agreed to adopt Thorn, immediately spotted him in the very top crate. She couldn't wait to take him home.

Like almost all of the dogs, Thorn was very scared. Once Sally got him home, he was exhausted after the long journey and slept for 24 hours straight.

At first, Thorn was very anxious and insecure. However, with help from Sally's corgi cross Rosie, Thorn has settled in well to his new home. Rosie and Thorn romp together like puppies, and, after Rosie, his favourite things are food, long walks, food, riding in the car and of course food. He has even been in a fashion parade, strutting his stuff down the 'dogwalk' in a fundraiser for the Waikanae SPCA.

Billie & Charley

On 22 February 2011, Monique would normally have been at home in Sumner with her two Labradors, Billie and Charley. However, on that particular day, Monique's son's school had finished early so they were in Ballantynes in the central city when the quake struck and Billie and Charley were home alone.

As Billie and Charley relaxed inside, the shaking started. Suddenly, a 4 tonne boulder came hurtling through the back wall of the second-storey bedroom, just missing the bed that Charley usually lay on. It crashed through the floor into the lounge downstairs and then out the ranch slider and through the fence, before continuing on down the hill.

The boulder only just missed Billie and Charley. They desperately wanted to get out of the house but they were trapped inside by rubble, broken glass, twisted window frames and debris.

A neighbour who had been home at the time of the quake and another boy who went to the same school as Monique's son had heard the boulder hit the house. They knew no one was home so went to check on the damage. They could hear the dogs barking inside.

The kitchen window had popped out, so they climbed in through the hole and lifted Billie and Charley out of the window to safety. As soon as their legs hit the ground the dogs fled, escaping through the hole in the fence created by the boulder.

Later that afternoon, a neighbour found Billie and Charley with some other neighbourhood dogs, all hiding in the bushes at the bottom of the valley. The neighbour took Billie and Charley back to his house for the evening. Monique's husband, Alistair, was able to make it home later that night, but Monique and her three children were stranded for the night on the other side of the city.

After the quake, Monique, Alistair and their family couldn't go back to live in their house because of the danger of falling rocks, so they stayed with Monique's parents. Charley was a nervous wreck. Every time an aftershock hit, she would run under someone's legs and quiver with fear. She even bit Monique, and on a separate occasion Alistair, when they frightened her by waking her suddenly. Monique worried that she might have to put Charley down if she made a habit of biting people, but the vet explained that she was just stressed and would calm down with time. Billie was not so affected by the aftershocks.

After three weeks of staying with Monique's parents, the family miraculously found a rental house in Redcliffs that would allow them to have Charley and Billie. Unfortunately, Monique's two cats were not allowed, so they stayed at the old abandoned house. Ever since then, Monique has gone every day to feed them. The house is currently zoned green but has been red-stickered, so they still don't know whether they will ever be able to return.

Crystal

Crystal, also known as Piggy for the snuffling noise she makes, is a four-year-old French bulldog that lives in Oamaru with Alison and her five Dalmatians and border collie. On 22 February 2011, it was unfortunate timing that Crystal was in Christchurch, being inseminated at the vet clinic.

Sam, who had bred Crystal and was looking after her while she was in Christchurch, was working at St George's Hospital near the city centre, so she quickly realised how severe the situation was. As the city slowly shut down, she was terrified that Crystal might be trapped at the vet clinic. Sam tried to make her way from the hospital into the city, but at Bealey Avenue she ran into a police cordon and couldn't go any further. She had no choice but to return home to Rangiora and think of another way to get Crystal out. Sam's husband suggested that they should get up at four the next morning and try to rescue her before security got too tight.

They left Rangiora well before dawn, but it was very difficult getting into the city because of all of the closed bridges. Eventually they managed to make it to the vet clinic, which luckily was just outside the cordon. When they arrived, the clinic was locked and they decided they would wait until 7 a.m. to see if anyone would show up before they resorted to breaking in.

Just 10 minutes later, Emma, one of

the vet nurses, arrived at the clinic. She had stayed the night with her brother nearby, as she couldn't make it back to her house in Rangiora. Ironically since Sam and her husband had just come from there, they were able to tell Emma the best route to get home.

When Sam went inside the vet clinic, it was pitch dark without power, and smelled cold and clammy, like a house that hadn't been opened or aired for weeks. She eventually found Crystal in a huge kennel in the middle of the clinic. Her eyes were like saucers, big even by bulldog standards, and Sam could sense her overwhelming fear.

Crystal had been through such a stressful experience that Sam and Alison never thought the insemination would work. However, two months later five beautiful pups were born. One became a show champion in Australia, one went to live with Sam and became a New Zealand champion, and the other three are now much-loved pets.

Crystal went on to have other litters and continues to enter shows, although Alison has modest expectations as Crystal has a lopsided ear after being bitten by another dog when she was just a pup. She is also beginning agility training and loves flying over the jumps. But her favourite thing of all is hanging out with Alison and her best mate, Izi the Dalmatian.

Kiwi

Before the 22 February 2011 quake, Blair and his guide dog Kiwi had a daily routine: they walked to the bus stop, took the bus into the city and went to work in the Telecom building on Hereford Street. Kiwi sat under the desk while Blair manned the phones. At some stage during the day, Blair would take a break and they would go for a walk by the Avon River.

When the February earthquake hit, it had been just another normal day. Blair was on the phone with a customer on the West Coast, and Kiwi was curled up under the desk. Blair jumped from his chair and nudged Kiwi aside so he could squeeze in beside him. When the shaking stopped, Blair reached up and put on his headset just in time to hear his customer say, 'Oh my god.'

The sirens soon started and Blair knew they had to get out of the building. He thought it might take a crowbar to get Kiwi out from under the desk, but pretending they were simply going about their daily routine calmed him. Blair was careful not to walk any faster than normal and Kiwi seemed to remember his routine despite all of the chaos happening around them.

At the top of the stairs, Blair and Kiwi were told to wait, lumped in with all of the others in the building with disabilities to be evacuated as a group. Blair debated with himself about whether to just leave, but he waited for a while and was glad he did, as a friend soon brought him his

abandoned backpack.

They eventually made it down the stairs and were on the street when the first large aftershock hit. The street was buckled so severely that Kiwi had to climb over knee-high bumps. Blair had to kneel down to feel the new landscape of the once familiar street.

Blair and Kiwi joined a group of colleagues and began slowly drifting through the city, unsure exactly where they should go or how they would get home. They reached Oxford Terrace by the Avon River, and Kiwi started eating grass. Blair recalls saying, 'Maybe he's doing it for comfort —it's something familiar he can remember.' A woman passing nearby murmured that maybe everyone should start eating grass, and Blair retorted that people who gain comfort from grass generally don't eat it! It was a rare spark of humour in an unbearably sombre afternoon.

As they moved, Blair's colleagues described the scenes of devastation around them. There were lots of dogs running free. There was a woman wrapped only in a mattress protector. And there were crumpled buildings and frantic people everywhere.

Eventually they made it to a colleague's car and it took them two hours to drive down Bealey Avenue to Linwood. Kiwi just sat calmly at Blair's feet, trusting fully that as long as he was with Blair, he would be safe.

When they finally reached their home in Prebbleton about 5.30 p.m., Kiwi went straight to bed, exhausted from the emotion and anxiety of the day.

After February, Blair's work moved to Addington and suddenly their daily routine became much more complicated. Kiwi did some re-training to learn the new terrain, but it was unsafe, with lots of carparks scattered among the business units and no footpaths. It was decided that it would be better for Blair to work from home.

Now that Blair is at home during the week, Kiwi has lost most of his day-to-day guiding work. Guide dogs need this daily practice to remain good at their jobs, so now Blair and his family are starting to talk about what Kiwi will do when he retires. He's almost 12 years old now, and soon it will be time for his working life to come to an end.

Acknowledgements

We would like to thank all of the dog owners and dogs that contributed to this project. In particular, the USAR dog handlers were extremely generous with their time. Carolyn Press-MacKenzie, founder of HUHA, was also very helpful in tracking down the earthquake refugee dogs in Wellington, and Trisha Stewart of K9 Rescue and Rehoming helped locate several earthquake dogs in Christchurch.

We would also like to thank the Random House team that believed in our idea and helped it become a reality. In particular, thanks to Jenny Hellen, Stuart Lipshaw, Sarah Ell and Carla Sy.

Laura thanks her husband, Will, who first dreamt up the *Quake Dogs* idea, and for his endless patience and support while I focused on the dogs. Craig would like to thank his husband Chris for his patience and for driving him to many of the photoshoots without question or complaint. I couldn't have done it without you.